I, Radical

God's Radical Business
through an Ordinary Man

Buck Jacobs

Founder of The C12 Group

with Kenneth R. Overman

Contents

Introduction

If you are a Christian, the information in this book may well prove to be the second most important you will ever receive. You might think, *That's a very bold statement!* I agree, but it is based on my belief that you and I have much in common.

Of course we have many differences, but there are four commonalities that cover the major roles and arenas of all of our lives: faith, marriage, children, and profession. Most of our lives are spent focused on these four major pieces. Am I right?

There is one more thing we have in common as Christians that you may not be as familiar with. My studies show that less than 20% of Christians are familiar with the term, the "Bema Judgment Seat of Christ." Many Christians do not understand the meaning and significance of the term. The Bible says: "We must all appear at the Judgment Seat of Christ so that each one may receive what he has done in the Body, whether good or bad" (2 Corinthians 5:10). It goes on to say that we build on the foundation of our lives in Christ with wood and hay, or gold and diamonds (1 Corinthians 3:10–15), which represent our works in this life. It says that fire will test our works, and that only some of them (the works) will pass the test. The works that pass will provide us with rewards, but those that burn up will mean loss.

Works are what we do, how and why we do them, and the way we invest our time and efforts. They have to do with how we fulfill God's plan for us (Ephesians 2:10). Works are not about going to Heaven ... Jesus has already settled that for those who trust in Him. Works are about things we do while living on earth, which will affect aspects of our eternal experience.

The bottom line is that our business and what we do with it here on earth impacts us for eternity.

God has only one set of values and only one purpose for leaving us here after we are saved, and that doesn't change. The problem is that our culture has taught us that our businesses, and how we run them, are somehow not a part of the equation. We have been told that we can't (or shouldn't) mix our faith with our business. That is simply not true. The real truth is that we cannot separate them … that is, unless we want to be seen as living hypocritically, using different value systems depending on our surroundings, like so many professing Christians unfortunately do.

Here is another thing that we have in common. True success for you and me will be found in finishing our race well, in passing through the judgment of our works and hearing Jesus say, "Well done!" But will He be able to say, "Well done" about the way we live our lives at work? What are we doing that has eternal significance at work? In the context of the lives we live, how do we keep our focus on the eternal when we are so impacted by the daily pressures of life and work? And how can we integrate the present physical life with the eternal one in a way that is real and practical? Is there a way to live in both dimensions at the same time and be successful at both? I hope this book will provide a basis for your own study that answers these questions.

Tielhard de Chardin, the French philosopher and Jesuit priest, said, "We are not physical beings who have occasional spiritual experiences. We are spirit beings who are having a temporary physical experience." Think about that. We all know that our trip on this planet is temporary and that it will end. But as Christians we also believe that when it ends we will go on to Heaven, to eternal life with Jesus. But have you ever wondered why we are left here after we are saved? Is it punishment? Can we become more saved as time passes? Can our performance make God love us more? No, none of these things are true. We are here because God has chosen us to be His ambassadors to the world around us.

The point is that as Christians we will go to Heaven, and a significant portion of what we experience *there* will be determined by what we do *here*. There will be an accounting for each of us, and that accounting will be done individually and will cover our role as stewards of all the resources we have been given.

I once met with Max DePree, CEO and Chairman of the Herman Miller Corporation. He asked me what I did. I replied, "I help Christians integrate their faith into their business." He thought for a moment and kindly responded, "Buck, don't you have that backwards? Shouldn't we be bringing our business to our faith? Isn't our faith our true center?" I knew he had nailed it. Of course our faith is the center of our lives and we should see everything else in light of it, including our work.

A Christian who runs their business with only the world's view of success is like a confused golfer who tees off facing backwards; he can hit every shot perfectly from that point, but he will never reach the green or succeed. You might have had success in your business from the world's perspective, but maybe you sense there must be more. Maybe you've thought, *There must be more than just financial success. There must be more meaning, more significance* than you have experienced so far. Maybe you've never considered your business as a part of your eternal purpose. Or maybe you've been keeping your head down and hard at it, and just now you've begun to wonder if this is all there is.

The C12 Group is an organization of Christian CEOs and owners, designed and facilitated by Christian CEOs and owners. So we get it. C12 is all about building great businesses. In fact, we are a for-profit business ourselves, based on a fee-for-service commercial model that requires we provide a value for the time and money invested by business professionals expecting a return. We are challenged in every way that you are, but we know there is a greater purpose. What de Chardin said above is true. We are focused on being the best of both worlds: building excellent businesses as evidenced by world-class benchmarks, and guided by biblical principles and focused on life's most important priorities.

C12 Group members find time-tested ways to enhance success in both dimensions, for here and in the hereafter, and help each other learn and stay focused, based on an integrated, Christ-centered worldview. But we don't do it alone. Thousands of CEOs, owners, and presidents of businesses are C12 members and alumni. They can testify of C12's extreme value to their businesses and their lives. This has been accomplished through learning and interaction with peers in a professional, focused, proactive, confidential, Christ-centered environment.

I invite you to read through these pages to gain insight to The C12 Group's origins. And if you're not a member, please pray about becoming involved. You will discover our distinctive and uncommonly focused approach that equips truly successful servant leaders of businesses of all types and sizes. Then you can dive into our website, which is crammed with information. Most of all, if you're leading an established business, we ask you to come to a local meeting as our guest. I hope you all enjoy this journey into the background of C12.

May God bless you on your journey to reach your best potential fruitfulness in Christ Jesus.

Buck
July 2014

Prologue

Tampa, Florida – September 2001, in a Private Boardroom

"Excuse me, would you repeat that, please?"

It took the speaker standing at the head of the conference table several awkward seconds to respond to the question. The man at the other end of the table asked again.

"I said, what you're telling us about the business is impressive, but how is your family doing?"

Again the speaker hesitated while the question hung in the air like grainy smoke from a backed-up fireplace. I glanced at Don. His face was alert, his eyes wide. We all waited for the response.

***

It was a cloudless afternoon in early fall of 2001. Fifteen of us were gathered around the comfortable boardroom of the Tampa Palms Country Club in North Tampa, Florida, for the monthly C12 Group meeting. At this particular meeting, a man named Don Barefoot was there at my invitation. Don was at an inquiring place in his career, searching for God's will for the rest of his life. We had spent most of the day before discussing the C12 concept, and I described to Don how C12 had developed in the nine years since we started, and what our vision for the future looked like. C12 had grown to a wonderful level considering we had never really made an effort to grow, and we were at a point where we sought a leader who could take the existing organization to the next level—into the next century.

Don had literally appeared out of nowhere, but he'll discuss his perspective later in the book. Anyway, in sync with the leading of the Spirit and timed with Don's search for God's direction in his life, I decided it would be a good thing if he attended a C12 Group meeting so he could see what it was all about. During that meeting we met with a group of distinctly Christian CEOs and business owners. Their businesses ranged from a billion-dollar publicly traded company on the high end, to a small pest control business with eight employees at the lower end. This kind of mix—a picture of diversity in the Body of Christ even among this specialized gathering—is typical of our C12 Groups. From large to small companies, they were manufacturers, service providers—businesses of all types and sizes. In short, this was a typical day.

At 9:00 AM, our local C12 Chair, Scott Hitchcock, called the meeting to order. We proceeded through the normal agenda that C12 had developed over its 10-year history. There were a lot of good conversations with some laughter around the table, mixed with poignant, open sharing that led to prayer. This mix of conversation almost always leads to a level of intimacy among the group members, ushering in a most powerful sense of God's presence. Such expressions of trust and vulnerability among members are what set a C12 encounter apart from other professional business forums that I've experienced. Yes, this meeting looked like it would turn out to be a typical C12 Group monthly meeting.

The morning was focused on a devotion, prayer, accountability reporting, and study sessions that covered both business and ministry development. After lunch, we came to the time when one of the members makes an in-depth presentation of their business to the group. The presenter for the month describes their current business and plans going forward, and gives an account of their stewardship in three areas: team development, financial development, and ministry development. Then they relate their specific issues, opportunities, and challenges to the group and ask a few key questions. In this format the presenter seeks the counsel and advice from the members in an open discussion.

The presenting member for that day was a well-respected CEO of the billion-dollar enterprise mentioned above. He took his position at the head of the table. He opened his talk by pointing out that he was happy to see the members, looked forward to their input, and went on to make his presentation. It was, of course, professionally prepared and well delivered. He related that his businesses had grown, that a number of successful acquisitions had taken place, and so forth. Overall, it was a glowing report that would have been the envy of all in attendance. That's when the gauntlet came down in the middle of his speech.

"What you're telling us about the business is impressive, and we could spend the next 45 minutes discussing specific business issues. But since you have a great team focused on these things, I really want to know how your family is doing."

The abrupt question was asked in the speaker's mid-sentence. It came from the owner of the eight-person pest control business. The speaker stopped cold and stared at the man, unable to respond for several seconds.

"Well," he said, clearing his throat, "I think we're doing fine."

When he was about to continue, another member broke in. "So, how often do you have dinner together as a family during the week?"

The speaker paused, his body visibly stiffened. "I … I can't remember the last time we did that. Five of our kids are teenagers and three have cars. My wife also runs a business and serves on a couple local boards. And you know my schedule …"

The other member continued his pursuit. "Is there anyone home when the kids return from school each day? Do you even know where they are?"

The speaker shook his head and became visibly red-faced.

"Brother, we only get one chance to raise our kids. How about your relationship with your wife? Are you praying with her and having a quiet time with her daily? How about family devotions?" the same member asked.

The speaker's eyes narrowed. "No."

"And are you able to attend the events of the six children you have?" The group was well aware of the fact that there were six children—preteen and teens.

"Well," the speaker replied, "some of them, but not all of them."

It went on from there. The group continued to ignore the obvious success of his business and instead focused on the real needs in this member's life ... and heart. Their questions were not intended to hurt or harm, because by then they knew each other well and had *earned* the right to ask such probing questions—questions delivered from hearts and perspectives of genuine concern. This "iron sharpening iron" feature is a focus of The C12 Group concept.

***

That was Don's first day in what could be called a typical C12 Group meeting in a typical setting. The exchange Don witnessed could only have taken place within the context of two important factors: transparency and trust.

We have always tried to establish the best physical locations for our C12 Groups, which will provide a safe and refreshing break from the daily grind. They are typically in very nice boardroom-type settings—usually a country club—while others might be in a private meeting room of a hotel. Either way, they are in a place where honesty and emotion can be shared openly and in complete privacy.

The trust factor is huge, so one of the core commitments of members of every group is to hold in strict confidence everything that takes place. Confidentiality is also one of the most important *benefits* of membership—being able to be free and transparent while assured of a high level of trust and honesty within the group. The day that Don visited was a day when—as with all C12 Groups—prayer needs were expressed. The members' requests and prayers were candid, open, and focused. Afterwards there was a time for sharing and praise reports, with thanksgiving and glory given to God for His provision. Sometimes a Scripture verse was shared to enhance a topic, give direction, or to affirm another member.

I pointed out to Don that within the diversity of the Tampa group there were also unity in Christ and many commonalities, which is true for all C12 Groups across the country. In fact, these similarities apply to Christian businesses throughout the world. There are men and women leaders who have advanced in their spiritual walk to the point where they realize that what they do with their professional life is an integral part of their Christian life. They have realized that God is not just a God of Sunday morning and Wednesday night, but He is God of the entire week. They help each other see the "one life" they share under Christ's lordship on a 24/7 basis, from the eternal perspective.

C12 tends to draw people who are serious in two areas of their lives. First, they're serious about growing strong businesses as stewards of what God has entrusted to them. Second, they're serious about glorifying God through their business. Thus the C12 motto: *"Building Great Businesses for a Greater Purpose."*

Of course, in every group there are all levels of spiritual maturity, with tremendous diversity of denominational expressions. So our doctrinal statement is very simple: "Jesus Christ is Lord of all, the Bible is totally true, and God has a plan for every believer's life, and that includes their business." Beyond these three foundational perspectives, C12 is nondenominational and nondoctrinal.

That day, we observed quite a mix of personalities and backgrounds around the table; people at every stage of their business life were investigating what God has for them. Don had been given a snapshot of the people and the process that make up a typical C12 Group meeting.

***

As the dialogue progressed, the speaker overcame his embarrassment and began to open up. He saw how the more important issues in his life were lacking, and how he had been making provision for all the things he perceived that his business needed, while trying to fit the needs of his wife and family *around* the business. He also realized that doesn't work very well and it ignores God's clear priorities.

As time went on, the speaker became humbled and somewhat broken. When the meeting adjourned, he told the group he was very grateful for their helping him grasp what he really needed to hear. He realized that life and business weren't only about two more points to his top or bottom line, but how other priorities—God's priorities—are much more important, and he had been slighting them.

After the meeting, Don and I spent more time talking. He told me what, to him, was the most important part of the day. He said he was amazed at how the owner of a very small, totally unrelated business, had the courage to challenge the life of the CEO of a much larger, publicly traded company. Not only did the man have the courage to say it, but he was obviously guided by God's Spirit to put his finger on a key area of the member's greatest need in a very loving, firm way. Don said he'd never seen anything like it in any group, ever. He had never seen leaders of large organizations who so often suffered from not having people speak into their life, become transparent and able to hear the truth in love … to allow *iron to sharpen iron.*

Today, Don is C12's extremely capable President and CEO. The meeting I just described was the vehicle God used to steer him to us, and since then C12 has continued to thrive and grow. But I'll let him tell the story in his own chapter at the end of this book.

For now, I'll tell you my story, and how C12 was born.

Chapter 1

I, Radical

I am a radical.

Many, if not most people, wonder why I am so passionate about my faith … why I can't just go along to get along, be like other Christians who aren't so … radical. Well, I can't. Even though there are times that I wish I could, I just can't.

Maybe it's because of the way it all started for me. There was a time when the whole idea of faith wasn't even a remote part of my life. Sunday mornings weren't about going to church; they were about recovering from Saturday night, or playing golf, or both. I believed there was a God somewhere, but I didn't know Him. He wasn't a part of my thinking or the way I lived my life. I lived for things I grew up believing were important: money and lots of it, friends, and being seen as successful. I wanted to be known as shrewd and tough, in charge, a man who could make things happen.

In my school years it was all about being an athlete, scoring touchdowns, making points, winning the conference, going to State, a scholarship, being popular, dating the most beautiful girls. When I left school it was about competing in business and climbing the ladder. The goals were basically the same—win and take no prisoners. The measure for success changed, yet the game was always the same. Compete, compare, be better than, have more than, be stronger, tougher, get farther than ….

I don't want to paint a totally dark picture of my growing-up years. While there certainly were bad times, there were a lot of good times as well. There was never any doubt in my mind that my mother and father loved me. They were actually wonderful people whose lives were caught up in the aftermath of World War II. And like many in their generation, they didn't handle their problems as well as they could have. But there was never a time that they didn't give me love and encouragement, even under difficult circumstances.

I grew up in the countryside of Crystal Lake, Illinois, in the 1940s and '50s. It was a wonderful time and place, with all kinds of sporting activities. I explored the hills and forests, hunted, fished, and played football and baseball with the kids in the neighborhood. My dad was always a supporter of my activities, and when I took up golf my mother used to caddy for me. She also kept score at every basketball game I played in. As an older brother, I had, and still have, a loving relationship with my brother and sister.

Nevertheless, when I look back—yes, there are some dark memories that I'll mention later in this book. But aside from that, I really loved my mom and dad. They did their very best. As I've grown older and have experienced problems and failure in my own life, I have realized how difficult it was for them in their lives.

By the age of 32 I was burned out. I was living in Italy, where I founded and ran a business. I had a big, beautiful villa (worth probably 2–3 million in today's dollars) in an exclusive gated village north of Rome, with the requisite Italian sports car—a Maserati—sitting in the driveway. I had already been President or CEO of three other businesses, earning an income that would have been in the top 1% in the world. By any standard, I had it all. I could have whatever money could buy and I bought it as fast as I could. My neighbors were some of the richest people on earth.

At a young age I had accomplished more than I ever dreamed. There was no more to get, and I knew it. It would only be more and I sensed that *more* wouldn't matter in any real way. Inside, I was empty and miserable. I was very angry and frustrated because somehow all I had worked for and accomplished still didn't work for me. I believed it would, and thought material success and recognition would bring happiness. It didn't.

In fact, the opposite was true. I had climbed the ladder of success, only to find that it was leaning against the wrong building. Worse yet, in my search for success I had deeply hurt others that I loved, as well as myself, and I couldn't take back the hurt. I was sick of the game and sick of myself. I thought, *If life is 30 more years of this—another relationship, a new business, a few points on the bottom line, new clothes, more jewelry, another whatever—I'm not interested.* I never considered giving up or ending my life, but I became cynical and negative to the point that no one wanted to be around me, especially when I had been drinking. In spite of all my success, life sucked.

I walked away from the business in Rome and started another with some friends in Denver, and then another in Los Angeles. I hoped a change of scenery would make a difference. It didn't. I truly didn't care about the new ventures; I simply threw money at them until I had no more to throw. I drank too much too often, and tried to make up for my discontent by acting out aggressively. Nothing helped. It only made the inner pain worse.

I don't believe that going into detail about all the things I did to try to fill the void would help this story. So I won't say more than this: Whatever you think it might have been, it was worse. People who know me today would never believe the things I did or the person that I was. To my knowledge I never killed anyone, but beyond that I have been guilty of the most sinful and obnoxious behavior you could imagine. Liar, cheater, thief, adulterer, drunkard … yes, I was all of these and more. I used people and manipulated them to my benefit. To me, the only sin was being caught, and that didn't happen much.

Inside, in a quiet place I didn't go very often, I felt heartsick and lost. I knew it was wrong but I didn't know what to do or how to do it. I'm not proud of this time in my life … in fact I'm very ashamed. But the truth is that even though I tried in some ways to be better, I was not a very nice person and I knew it.

Then came a day that for me was unlike any other. It was Sunday, November 18, 1973. My future wife, Bonnie, was on a trip visiting her mother in New Orleans. I got up late and when I turned on the TV to watch a football game, a church service came on instead. I had never watched a church service on TV before. I didn't go to church, nor did I think I had to. But when I heard the first few sentences of the pastor's sermon, I was riveted. I watched the entire program.

***

Looking back, I knew the process had begun the day before, on Saturday. I was idling around the condominium pool that morning and happened to watch two men playing backgammon. One was a well-known comedian that I recognized, and the other, a short little guy with one arm, that I didn't know but had seen around the pool. I didn't know how to play the game so I sat and watched them from about 20 feet away. They laughed and cursed and seemed to be having a great time. When the game finished, the comedian got up and left. The short man caught my eye and waved me over. He was very direct with me.

"So what's your deal?" he asked. "Are you rich?"

"No, I'm not rich … in fact I'm just about broke," I answered.

This was an unusual response, to say the least, because I never confided in anyone in those days. I always tried to put up a false front to look successful, even as I slid down the slope towards bankruptcy. But without thinking, I opened up to this unusual stranger. He introduced himself as Teddy Brooks.

"That girl I see you with, are you married to her?" he asked.

"No. I've been married twice and they didn't work out," I said.

"Are you nuts? Can't you see she loves you?" he said, looking me in the eye. "What's your big problem?"

For some unknown reason I poured my heart out to this stranger. I told him of my frustration, the failure of all my success to bring happiness, and how I had gone from being a golden-haired boy with the "Midas Touch" to a cynical and sullen man who couldn't get anything to work. Ted listened attentively and then said something I never imagined would come from a man I overheard swearing and cursing a few minutes before.

"You're a bright young man, Buck, and you have a lot going for you. But you need God in your life."

In spite of the unusual source, I knew his words touched me in a place I needed but never would have looked for, especially not by a swimming pool in Southern California.

"So, what should I do?" I asked.

"I don't know," he said, "but once when I was really down, a Jewish friend of mine told me to memorize three Psalms. I did and it seemed to help. Why don't you try that?"

I didn't know what he was talking about. "What are Psalms … you mean like in the Bible?"

"Yes." He paused and looked me in the eye. "Don't you have a Bible?"

"No." (I had never opened a Bible in my life.)

"Tell you what. I'll loan you one somebody gave me. It's in my apartment."

We went up to his apartment and he handed me a blue softcover Bible. He told me I could keep it. I thanked him and took the elevator up to my apartment, somewhat dazed by what had just happened. In the elevator, I thought of my best friend, Bob Mack, who had tried to tell me something about God and Jesus a few years earlier.

Bob and I have been best friends since we were 12, and our lives have been knit together in many ways. We competed against one another in grade school and we became teammates in high school. Bob played fullback and I played halfback. He was guard and I was forward. We dated girls who were friends. He took over his family business within months of my being elected president of our family business.

I should call Bob and ask him about God, I thought. But I realized I wouldn't want Bob to know about my financial condition, or that I needed anything. I immediately dropped the idea.

The elevator dinged open, and I went into my apartment. Inside the living room I was shocked to find a book on the coffee table by the sofa—a book Bob sent me after the last time we had seen each other. I'd had too much to drink at dinner and forgot to take the book. It arrived a few days later in the mail. I was embarrassed about how I had acted and just put it aside.

In fact, I never even read a bit of it and had forgotten all about it. In the meantime I had moved from Cedar Rapids to Minneapolis, then to Rome, Denver, and then Los Angeles. I don't ever remember packing his book or even seeing it before that day. But there it was on the table. I picked it up and read the title: *The Art of Understanding Yourself – An Invitation to Wholeness – And to Life Itself!,* by Cecil Osborne.

That afternoon I read the three Psalms Ted had marked for me in the Bible, and then I decided to read Bob's book. I opened the flyleaf and saw that his wife, Holly, had written "God's peace be with you, Bucky. Love, Bob and Holly." I still have the book. The title of the first chapter was "Your Lonely Self." I had never thought of myself as lonely, but I was drawn into the book. I stayed up almost all night and finished it.

There was much in the book I didn't understand. Many of the concepts presented are very familiar to me today, but were foreign at the time. The overarching message was that somehow it was possible to have a relationship with God, and people, that would be loving, accepting, and healing. The book featured many testimonies of the positive effects of small groups of Christians who met together to talk through their experiences and learn about a God who is love.

In the little bit I knew about God, I had never considered Him to be interested in me personally—at least not until after I died, when He would be waiting to punish me for my sins. I didn't have a problem believing I was a sinner who deserved to be punished … that part was easy. If there was a God and He had anything like the Ten Commandments for rules, I was toast.

The book described forgiveness in a way I had never heard, and the people who shared their stories seemed a lot like me. They carried guilt and regret for things they'd done or what had happened to them. Many shared how performance-based acceptance had warped their lives and how they felt that no matter what they did, it was never good enough. Some said their guilt came from their church experience that was all about keeping the rules, or from the judgmental attitudes of others. I didn't identify with all of them, but plenty enough to get a sense that they had something I didn't, and that I needed what they had.

I thought a lot about Bob and Holly that night. I had seen a change in their lives after they became Christians. It was change for good and although I had always respected them and admired their marriage, it seemed to get even better after what they described as a "born-again experience." Of course I had no idea what that meant and I even made fun of them when they tried to explain it to me. When I finished reading, I thought this must be at least part of what they were trying to tell me.

I finished the book and went to sleep thinking that I needed to become a Christian, without knowing how or what it meant. Did I need to join a church? If so, which one? I had taken instruction in the Catholic Church years before, but nothing I studied prepared me for a personal relationship with God. It seemed to be a bunch of rules that didn't make sense, and most of the Catholic people I knew seemed to ignore them anyway. If the old priest who instructed me had ever tried to tell me about Jesus as my personal Savior, I didn't get it. I tried to keep the rules for a while, but quickly broke them. Eventually I became discouraged and gave up on religion altogether; but I didn't give up on God. I knew He was there and I knew He would judge me. I just had no clue that He loved me.

I went to sleep not fully realizing all that had taken place in the space of 18 hours—up until I switched on the TV to the church program instead of football. It was 10:00 AM. I sat back and listened.

***

"Problems are an inevitable part of life," said the speaker with a kind expression, as he paced back and forth on the stage. The cameras followed him closely. "No matter who you are—Christian or not—problems will always come and go. No one can avoid them or live a life without them. And if you try to deal with them in your own strength, sooner or later they will break you down."

He had my attention. I had nothing but problems in my life: money problems, relational problems, health and lifestyle problems, career and direction problems. And most of all, purpose-for-living problems. Anxiety filled me whenever I thought about where to go or what to do with my life.

The pastor went on: "But I have good news for you today. God loves you and if you will give your life to Him in Jesus Christ, He will take responsibility for your life. And from then on, every problem will become an opportunity to see His love and power."

He said a lot more, but that was the essence of his message as I remember it. He explained that Jesus had come to the earth in the form of a man and died for my sins. He actually took the punishment that I deserved upon Himself and, by doing so, made it possible for me to be forgiven and to have a new life … to be born again. I had previously heard that Jesus died to take away the sins of the world, but that meant nothing to me personally. I still sinned, so I figured either I didn't count, or grace hadn't worked. But the speaker said it was a choice, a gift offered that must be accepted. He said the gift is offered to everyone, but not everyone takes it. I knew that I never had.

"And you can receive the gift of God's love and forgiveness right now, wherever you are," he said as the camera moved closer. "So if you're watching this on television, you can get on your knees right in your home and give your life to God. You can receive His Son and His forgiveness and the new life He offers you."

That was my answer! Without hesitation or embarrassment, I knelt down at the same coffee table where I found the book Bob had sent, and I prayed.

"Lord Jesus, if this is real and You want my life, You can have it and I will do whatever You want with the rest of it. Please forgive me, Jesus. I know that I am lost and have sinned. I am sorry, Lord, and I turn away from the life I have been living and give my life to You."

As I prayed I began to cry. I cried even as I wrote this. I can't help it. It has been over 40 years and that moment is *still* so real to me. In my mind's eye I am back in that apartment, crying and confessing my sin. I can see in my spirit, myself lying at Jesus' feet, and can still hear the words: "Jesus is the best friend I will ever have." Were those real words? Where did they come from? I don't know, but over the years Jesus has proven them to me over and over and over again. Jesus *is* my friend as well as my Lord and my Savior. Yes, He is the King of Kings and Lord of Lords … God in man … all of that and more. That was the morning when I began to know He is my friend, my best-ever friend.

I cried for a while until it stopped, and then sat back on the couch. When the message was finished, the program ended, and I wondered, *What just happened?* I couldn't explain, understand, or put it in words; somehow I knew my life had changed forever.

But what comes next? What do I do now? I spent the day in a kind of questioning wonder. *Was it all real? What should I do?*

That afternoon I went down to the pool, but no one was there. I rested in the sun, wondering, *What did it mean? What do I do next?*

It didn't take long for Jesus to begin to show me.

Chapter 2

The Way Appears – The "Grand Experiment" Begins

Bonnie returned from New Orleans late Sunday night. She'd had a few drinks on the plane, and under those circumstances I didn't want to try to tell her about how I gave my life to Jesus. Besides, I didn't know what I was going to say anyway, so I put it off until the next night.

As we sat at the table over dinner on Monday, I tried to explain all that had transpired on Saturday with Teddy, and on our couch the next day. I told her about the TV sermon, reading the book, the sermon, and that I had given my life to Jesus. And while I had no idea how, I told her that things were going to get better for us. At that time, my financial slide had fallen to the point of using the last of a collection of silver dollars that Bonnie used to buy groceries. My bank account had hit zero and my credit cards were about maxed out. My only reserve was a Visa card that I'd mysteriously received in the mail not long before and which I'd put aside to use only as a last resort.

I told Bonnie how I wanted to talk to Bob and Holly, but didn't have the guts to let them know how bad off I was. Just then, the phone rang. When I heard the voice on the other end of the line, I instantly knew that the deal I had made with Jesus the day before was real, and that my life would never be the same.

The voice said, "Buck? It's Bob."

No one on earth knew how much I had thought about Bob and Holly or how badly I wanted to talk to them. But God knew.

"When are you coming to Chicago again?" Bob asked.

I was stunned. Could this be happening? Was this my first test as a Christian? I wanted to lie to Bob and tell him I was too important and busy to come to Chicago—which is what I would have done if he had called on the previous Friday. But for whatever reason, the lie stuck in my throat and I said, "I won't be coming to Chicago anytime soon, Bob. I'm broke and I can't afford it."

"Don't worry about that, I'll send you a ticket. I really want to talk to you." He sounded excited. "Listen, Buck, I gave my business to Jesus about a year ago and He has given me some new products that are very exciting. I need help with sales and I'd like to talk with you about coming to work with us."

I choked up and could barely croak out my response. "Th-that would be great, Bob."

He heard the catch in my voice and asked, "What's wrong?"

"I just gave my life to Jesus yesterday."

Then it was his turn to choke up. "Holly and I have prayed for you every night for four years. Praise the Lord!"

My friend, the fullback and linebacker, and I, the halfback, wept and then rejoiced together.

"We have to talk," Bob said.

Within a week I was in Aurora, Illinois, meeting with Bob and his team. It was unbelievable. Bob had led his two partners to Christ over the past couple of years. I saw the enthusiasm and joy in their relationship and their excitement about what the future would bring. Bob asked me to join the company and build sales for a line of synthetic coolants called PTL products … PTL standing for "Praise the Lord."

I was amazed and excited. I would have gladly swept the floors for the chance to work with my friend and his team in a business that was trying to be what Bob described as a "Christian company." He didn't really know what that meant, and of course neither did I or the others, but the details weren't all that important at the time. Bob had gone through the process of being born again about four years earlier and had experienced great joy and peace in every area of his life, except the business. Business was always a hassle for him and it lurched from trial to crisis, to okay, and back again. But he'd never experienced the joy in the business that he had found in the rest of his life such as his family and church. He recognized that business was the one area he had never given to God. He had kept control of it for himself.

One day, in frustration, he got on his knees behind his desk and released the business to God. He told God that if he were to stay, God would have to be the owner and Chairman of the Board. Bob recognized that he had been living a separate life at work, using one set of values there and another at home with his family and at church. With that, Bob put it to rest. He would be a Christian all the time and if not, he'd find a place where he could— perhaps as a pastor, missionary, or a coach.

That was the turning point for Bob and for the business. The great thing about Bob (the fullback) is he has only one speed—charge! (a typical fullback). When he decides to do something, he goes for it with all he has. Thank God this was no different. Bob called it the "grand experiment." Could a business be Christian? Of course a business can't go to Heaven, but was the Bible relevant to daily business life? And if so, could a person be a business success and maintain a consistent Christian life? He committed to find out.

As Bob shared his vision, it resonated with me in ways I can't explain. What he shared was totally different from anything I had ever thought about, but in the deepest way I wanted to be part of it. We agreed that I would return to LA, pack up, and return to Aurora as soon as possible to start work. I flew back to LA and went about getting ready.

That unsolicited Visa card I had received in the mail and stuck away in a drawer became one of my first evidences of God's sovereign provision. When I received it I still had a little cash, so I stuck it away thinking maybe I'll need it someday. Well, that day had come. The bills were paid until the end of the month and Bob had given me $100 for meals and expenses. But I quickly found out that to rent a trailer to move the little bit of stuff we had to Illinois would cost way more than I had. I was discouraged, until I remembered the Visa card. I dug it out and was surprised to find it had a $600 open credit. That card got us to Illinois, with a bit to spare. I didn't know I needed a Visa card, but God did and He provided it. I began to learn that He is a Father who has all I need, to do all He asks.

We showed up at Bob's house in a snowstorm in early December. After a day or so to rest, we began to look at establishing our new life as part of a Christian business.

Chapter 3

Rising from the Ashes

Within two weeks of our arrival, Holly took Bonnie to a ladies' Bible study. Afterwards she led her to Jesus while they sat at her kitchen table. That's how we started our lives in Christ together, and we have been growing together in Him for 40 years. What a privilege!

We quickly found an apartment, and Bob cosigned a note at a local bank to help us get some working capital. The note was for $6,000, and I'm sure glad Bob hadn't yet learned the biblical principle about cosigning for another at that point, because I had nowhere else to turn. Later we learned that the Bible strongly discourages us from "giving surety," or cosigning, but neither of us understood it then. My starting salary was $13,000 per year—not even a good *month* a few years earlier—but I couldn't have cared less. It was what it was and I was thankful for it.

When Bonnie and I totaled our current debts and bills, the amount was $28,000. The apartment rent was $350 per month and our car payment was $225. My net pay was about $950 after taxes. We did the math and there wasn't much left for food or other expenses, let alone being able to reduce that debt. I contacted every one of our creditors and told them I had become a Christian. I promised I would send them whatever I could each month and that I would pay them in full. Most of them were not at all interested in my conversion, but they all agreed to let me try to work it out over time. It was around that time when I learned about tithing.

I'd heard a radio message about tithing, and I asked the pastor of the church we started to attend what that was. He told me it was the practice of taking the first 10% of a person's income and giving it to the church. I explained our circumstances to him and the fact that by tithing we would go further in debt each month. It seemed like "robbing Peter to pay Paul."

He said, "I understand, Buck. I didn't learn about tithing and the blessing of giving until I was already a seminary student living on the GI Bill, with a wife and three kids. I prayed about it and we started to tithe, even though it didn't seem possible. All I can tell you is that we never had too much but we always had just enough. We have continued to tithe to this day."

I went home and prayed about it and shared the idea with Bonnie. She agreed that we should go for it and start tithing, even if it looked like we would be bankrupt even faster. I remember praying, "Lord Jesus, if you want me to experience bankruptcy, I am willing. But from now on, we will give you the first tenth of all we earn."

That's exactly what we did. We never went bankrupt and, to my amazement, we paid off all our debts and stayed current with all our responsibilities. Within two and a half years, not only were we debt free, but we were blessed with our first child and were able to take two vacations. We did not lack for one single thing. Yes, there were lean times. I can remember when our big-time Friday night date was to pop some popcorn, light a candle, and listen to a Gaither LP on the stereo. I remember lying on the floor in our apartment, praying to God to provide the five dollars I needed for a new white shirt for work since I had spoiled all my others. He provided. We never went without anything then, or at any time in the 40 years since.

We have continued to give Jesus the first fruits of our gross income to this day. Even as we started C12 we gave the first 10% of our monthly billings, and continued to do so until we acquired investors. We have created the Jacobs Family Foundation, which will ultimately distribute all we have to the Kingdom's works. Our daughters and sons-in-law are co-trustees with Bonnie and me, and it is a blast to see God's resources directed to His people who need help.

God wasted no time showing how real He is and how He longs to be our Source—no matter how small the need. Once, I was praying for a new portable radio for an unusual friend of mine named Jimmy Walker. I met Jimmy through the men's Bible study at church. He was a resident in a local home for learning-disabled adults. Our church had a Sunday school class for a number of the residents at the home, and Jimmy would come to our men's Bible study group before going on to his class. The first thing I noticed about Jimmy was he ate all the donuts! He befriended me, and God used him in many very special ways in our lives over the next few years.

Jimmy, a Christian, carried a little radio with him as he roamed the city each day, always tuned to Moody Radio, a Christian station. One day he accidentally dropped and smashed the radio, and he was heartbroken. When he told me what had happened—with real tears in his eyes—I immediately wanted to replace the radio. But I also realized I couldn't, since I didn't have the money I imagined one would cost. Bonnie and I asked God to somehow provide a radio for Jimmy. That was on a Sunday.

On Monday when I got home from work, there were two very meaningful items in our mail. One was an ad from Walgreens drugstore highlighting a sale on transistor radios for $9.95. The other was a check for $9.95—an unexpected refund from a company where I had ordered a pair of inexpensive work shoes. They were out of stock and said they hoped I wouldn't mind a refund. I don't think I have ever been more excited by not receiving something I had ordered!

The next day we cashed the check, bought the radio, and gave it to Jimmy. The memory of the joy in his eyes will never leave me. Such a simple little thing, but we knew it was from God, to bless him. And I never reordered the shoes.

Jimmy had been in institutions from age 16, but somewhere along his journey he had met Jesus and they had a real friendship. He used to delight in calling me up to ask a Bible question. When I didn't know the answer, he would giggle and give it to me. Jimmy had a sweet spirit and he loved to walk over to our house for surprise visits. One day when he heard that we were going to have a baby (Sarah), he brought a bouquet of flowers for Bonnie. When she opened the door, he handed them to her with a big smile. The only problem was they still had their roots hanging on them … Jimmy had picked them from a neighbor's garden.

After Sarah arrived, Jimmy came to see her for the first time. Bonnie got her up from her nap and walked over to the couch where he sat.

She asked, "Would you like to hold her?"

I was a bit concerned because I didn't know what Jimmy would do. Bonnie gently laid Sarah in his huge hands.

"Oh, she's so cute," he said as twin tracks of tears rolled down his cheeks.

I can see it in my mind's eye today. The world called Jimmy "retarded," but Jesus calls him "friend." And because of Jesus, I do too.

Jimmy got cancer a few years later. After he was admitted to the hospital, he would call me to pray with him when the pain got to be too much. He always said it helped, but his simple trust helped *me* even more. Jimmy is with Jesus now. We'll pick up our friendship in Heaven, where I imagine he will still be listening to heavenly music and picking flowers for somebody.

***

About two weeks after I joined Bob at the Mack Company, I was in the office writing some data sheets for a new product when the phone rang. The caller asked for Bob, but he was skiing with his family that weekend and I was alone in the office. I asked if I could take a message or be of help to the caller.

"Who are you?" he asked.

I told him my name and that I had joined the company to help with sales.

"Maybe I should be talking to you," said Amos McDuff from Cape Cod. "I've been running some ads looking for reps, and I have a couple that I can't use who might be a fit for your company."

I told Mr. McDuff that would be wonderful, and that I would be happy to take their names and contact them. I didn't mention that although I was in charge of sales for the company I had no background in the business, no contacts in the field, and no idea where or how to start. He gave me the names of one man in Pittsburgh and another in Cincinnati. I was so excited I called them right then, even though it was Saturday.

I called the Pittsburgh contact first. He was at the office doing paperwork—on Saturday morning, as is so often the case with sales—and we had a cordial conversation. He agreed to see me when I could arrange a trip to Pittsburgh. I was elated.

I called the second man and got a very different response. His name was Bob Reicks.

When I told him our product line was industrial coolants and cleaners, he said, "Oh no, I had a line of those things once and they almost broke my company. I'm not interested."

In my newfound confidence (and maybe arrogance), I responded, "Then I guess you wouldn't be interested in earning $5,000 a month in commissions, like our rep in Cleveland with our PTL 710."

"PTL?" he asked. "What does that stand for?"

"It stands for Praise the Lord. We name all our products PTL."

"Are you a Christian?"

"I am. We are a Christian business."

"In that case, I'll be in your office Monday morning."

He was a man of his word and arrived in our office Monday morning. He turned out to be a wonderful Christian man who ran a manufacturer's representative agency called the Reicks Group. They had sales reps in Indianapolis, Ft. Wayne, Louisville, Dayton, and Cincinnati—the very heart of the geography we were hoping to penetrate. And they were calling on prime customers in the area. We quickly reached an agreement that gave him the rights to sell PTL products. That day, a great friendship and a mutually beneficial business relationship began.

I called Mr. McDuff to thank him; he wasn't in. In fact, we never heard from him again. Would he have otherwise called back on Monday to talk to Bob? Maybe, maybe not … we'll never know.

But that call launched me on what we later called the "milk route." I travelled by car from Aurora to Indianapolis, Ft. Wayne or Dayton, and to Louisville or Cincinnati each week. Several great things came from the milk route.

First, it was about 1,000 to 1,200 miles a week of driving time and I had lots of hours to listen to the radio. I found Christian stations all along the route and listened to wonderful Bible teachers like J. Vernon McGee and others. I also heard preachers like Jimmy Swaggart, as well as the music of Andraé Crouch and the Gaithers. Most of these names mean nothing to younger people these days, but they were my teachers five days a week on the road. They all pointed me to Jesus and helped me begin my journey as His disciple.

A second and very personal thing that God began in my life was to put me in a position where I knew I was (and still am) inadequate. I could then watch Him produce results that even a hardhead like me could not take credit for. Things would occur where I had to recognize that I couldn't take credit for what happened and there was no other explanation than "God did that!"

For example, I had never set foot in a chemistry class and never had any training in industrial coolant sales. I didn't know how difficult it was to break into a large coolant account. In fact, I was about one day ahead of our five salesmen with the information we'd share, and that made me the expert. Ha! I presented a silly Polaroid picture of some goldfish swimming in a fish tank, with a sign in the front that said "1 PPM PTL-710." I used two Gerber baby food jars—one with a sample of used PTL-710 (clear stuff) and the other with a sample of our competitor's soluble oil product (ugly stuff). Can you imagine? Our reps and I called on engineers and buyers at Ford, Chrysler, GM, International Harvester, and all the giants in metalworking. We spoke with R&D chemists who had PhDs in chemistry—any of whom could have shown me to be a fool.

But they never did. In fact, they began to buy in shorter sales cycles ... unheard of at the time. In a year, that little milk route was producing 40% of our revenues. I knew it was *in spite* of me rather than *because* of me. God was proving Himself as the sovereign Provider that I have found Him to be. And that was only the beginning. He also provides even in the darkest of times.

Sometime later that year, on a Saturday morning after breakfast, I called the office to share the week's events and talk with Bob. The phone line was busy, which was unusual since we had three incoming lines. It continued to be busy for about a half hour. The plant was only a half mile from our apartment, so I ran over to see what Bob was up to. As I turned the corner to drive down the street to the office, I saw a fire truck pulling away from our plant. When I got closer I saw that a fire had occurred in our building. Later I found out that an arsonist had squirted gasoline under the front door and torched us.

The entire front office area was in ruins ... scorched and then drenched by the water used to put out the fire. Bob was there, along with several others, and we stood in stunned silence looking at the devastation. Eventually someone asked, "What can we do?" The company had no fire insurance, no ability to borrow, and no cash surplus. The situation looked hopeless.

Earlier that week I had read a book titled *Shaping History through Prayer & Fasting*, by Derek Prince. The author explained the historic biblical relationship between fasting and prayer, and offered some modern-day examples. One example that particularly touched me was the story of a small church in England during the dark days of World War II. It was a time when it seemed certain that Hitler's Nazi forces would cross the English Channel and overrun England. At that point it appeared that nothing could stop the onslaught of the powerful German army. The church was a small congregation and it didn't seem like there was anything they could do.

One of the church members reminded the others of events in Bible history when God used supernatural means to defend Israel, when small forces prevailed over much greater armies. One example was the battle of Jericho, when Joshua led a small group marching around the fortified enemy, blowing trumpets. His suggestion was their church shouldn't focus on what they couldn't do, but on what they *could* do—they could pray and call out to God.

They established a system of constant, 24-hour prayer, and added fasting as well. Throughout each day, at least one member would be at the church praying and asking God to deliver them, while others fasted. A very interesting, specific request in the prayer was that God would send a "deluding spirit" on the enemy and confuse them. They put their plan to action.

Shortly after that, Hitler made what history judges as one of the mistakes—if not *the* decisive mistake—that turned the course of the war. He invaded Russia. In doing so, he diluted his forces and sent some of his best troops into a prolonged and costly disaster that culminated in their defeat and retreat. Of course no one can prove this was God's response to that little group's prayer. But no one can prove it wasn't, either. Hitler's action was by any measure a colossal and devastating decision—irrational at least and God-induced at best.

I told my friends about the book and the example as we stood in front of the smoking building. They immediately jumped on the idea, and we agreed to pray. On each Wednesday we added fasting to our prayer as well. We held hands in the parking lot and again lifted the business to God, saying that it was His and if He wanted it to continue, we would look to Him as our only hope. It seemed that as we prayed, our spirits lifted. Moments later, a man drove up in a pickup truck.

"I see you've had a problem. What are you going to do for an office?" the man asked.

"We don't know," I said.

None of us had gotten that far in our thought process.

The man thought for a moment. "Well, I have a construction trailer," he said, "and I just finished a job and don't need it for a while. I could tow it onto the vacant lot next door and you could have a phone line hooked up this afternoon. Your customers would never know you've had a problem."

The possibility jump-started our plans and we readily agreed.

Later as we looked through the building, we realized that almost all of our furniture was steel. And although scorched and with some of the padding burned off the chairs, they could be scrubbed, covered, and made useful for the short term. Most of the files and paper had been burned or were water damaged, but the desks and chairs could be salvaged. We went to work.

The company had no fire insurance and no ability to borrow funds to rebuild. As we worked with steel-wool pads and soap, cleaning a few desks and chairs, we understood that we had deep financial needs with no way to deal with them. Even though God had provided a temporary office and some furniture, we had no cash resources to repair the building or replace what had been lost.

Fortunately, there was a firewall between the office and manufacturing area, so we did have some inventory of raw material for the short-term supply of existing customers. But we couldn't divert cash from the purchase of new materials to pay for the needed repairs. Like many small businesses, we were running too close to the edge and had no financial cushion. The more we thought about it, the bleaker our long-term situation appeared. We didn't know how we would survive even beyond the current month.

As a Christian business, we were aware of our need to honor our debts and pay our creditors. So we agreed to a new compensation system to try to deal with our obligations. The four corporate leaders would take no salary during the month, but would wait until the end of the month to see if we made a profit—enough profit to pay our debts and continue. If we succeeded we would split the profit equally and move on to another month and so on, until we either failed or were able to return paying regular salaries.

After that bleak Saturday and the decisions we made that day, amazing things began to happen. For me, an early event was one that I hadn't considered. On the days when we were fasting I'd often take customers to lunch or dinner. How could I explain to them why I sipped water while they enjoyed a steak? I was intimidated at first, but these situations provided an opportunity to tell them about the "grand experiment" of trying to do business based on biblical principles as a Christian company.

I learned something very valuable, something I have often applied ever since. Others don't mind when we tell them what we believe—in fact, they like to do business with people who have convictions and are willing to try to live by them. They were okay as long as I didn't try to tell them what they should believe, or preach to them. Over many years, real friendships have developed this way. Of course I listened to them as well, since they often shared their own experiences and faith stories.

Those were the days of the Arab oil embargo, when lines were a mile long at the pumps. Oil-based chemicals were allocated and some were hard to get. Somehow, others learned we had a supply of a particular chemical that we had purchased in hopes of a big order that had never materialized. People began to call us, asking to buy our chemicals at four or five times the price we paid—an unexpected and timely cash infusion for the business. At the same time, we received orders from the milk route that we hadn't expected to get so soon. All in all, that month we had the highest sales and the highest profit in the history of the company. There was enough to pay the bills and enough to keep each of us paid for another month. The next month passed with similar results, so we kept praying and fasting. It was exciting. We saw things happen almost daily that showed God to be able and willing to meet our needs as we honored and trusted Him. After a few months we were back in our building.

Our compensation plan changed again, but rather than going back to straight salary as before, I was given a smaller salary with a commission on sales from the milk route. It seemed that it would work out about the same, but God had a better plan. The sales from the milk route doubled, and then doubled again. Within a few months I was earning twice what I had before the fire. I never asked for a raise, or even thought about it. That was the pattern for the 10 years that I worked with Bob. I learned to look to God to set my pay. In fact, in 40 years I have never asked anyone else for a cent. And for much of that time I had no salary or guaranteed source of income.

We never learned who set the fire to the building or why, but we learned things that are so much more valuable. The devil meant the fire as an act for evil, but God turned it on him and used it for good that continues to this day. Those early days of learning to trust in God as our Source were the foundation on which all of our lives have been built.

In the next couple of years the business continued to grow, and we saw miracle after miracle of God's provision in the midst of it all. The milk route flourished largely through the Bob Reicks Group. Our other accounts that had been threatened in various ways also stayed with us. Finally, during those pivotal two and a half years and in ways that I can't explain, Bonnie and I found ourselves out of debt and we began to save money … hopefully, to buy a house one day.

Chapter 4
While All That Was Going On ...

At the time God was doing amazing things for the company, Bonnie and I became very involved in a small evangelical Congregational church. While there, we learned His Word and grew in our faith. He used many resources and experiences to lead us on. One resource was to attend a seminar called "The Institute of Basic Youth Conflicts," taught by Bill Gothard. It was a deep and broad study of fundamental principles of biblical living. The class was taught in the evenings during the week and all day Saturday.

One study evening when I returned to O'Hare Airport after a day trip on business, I forgot where I had left my car. I needed to find it quickly if I were to make the class on time. When I got to the humongous O'Hare parking garage, I realized I didn't remember where my car was or even on which floor I'd parked it. I shot an arrow prayer to God, asking, "What floor?"

I didn't hear an audible voice, but got the impression to go to the sixth floor. I went to the nearest elevator and got off on that floor, but when I walked down a few rows I stopped. I realized I had no idea where to look. Frustrated, I looked to the left and down the row I was standing next to and, there, about halfway down and still quite a distance from me, I saw a car with its taillights blinking. It was my car, with the emergency lights flashing! It had been there since early morning and I hadn't turned them on. Even if I had, the battery would have been long dead 10 or 11 hours later. I tried the ignition and it started right away. You can judge for yourself what happened, but I knew then it was God, and I still do. I drove 70 miles and walked into the class just as it started.

Beth's Story

One of the greatest blessings that happened as a result of the Grace of God in my life was moving back to the Chicago area and being near my first daughter. Beth is the daughter of the marriage that I had ruined and left five years earlier. Still, Beth and I have always connected in ways that have blessed my life ... ways I don't deserve. I had given her every reason to resent or hate me by leaving her and her mom, but she never did. I had no idea how she would respond to me with my new life in Christ, and my new marriage. She began to visit with Bonnie and me on weekends, and she never showed the least of what would have been well-deserved resentment. Her sweet spirit has always found room for me, and I treasure her for it.

About six months after our move to Illinois we learned that Bonnie was pregnant. We began to think about life in a different way. Honestly, things were happening so fast in so many areas of our lives that we really hadn't planned for a family. While we were surprised, we were very happy to learn that planning would no longer be an option. We were excited, and I was particularly blessed because Beth was also excited for us. She has shown me so many times what grace, with skin on, looks like.

One time when Beth had come to spend the weekend, a potentially difficult situation arose. Beth's mom was firm about my having her home on time after our visits, and I wanted to honor her by complying without fail. I understood she was a bit skeptical of my new life and she had every reason to be. But I didn't blame her and it was never a problem until this particular day.

While I prepared to gather Beth and her things, Bonnie told me she had extremely painful cramps and nausea, and asked me to pray for her. Just when I asked God to heal her and relieve her pain, she immediately went into the bathroom, thinking that she might throw up. I felt conflicted; I knew Bonnie needed me, but I also knew if I didn't leave almost immediately I would get Beth home late. I shot an arrow prayer to the Lord. I called Beth's mom to explain the situation and asked for an extra hour. She kindly agreed. Then I told Beth that Bonnie was ill and that she could watch TV while I tried to help Bonnie.

In those days there was a Sunday night TV program sponsored by the Full Gospel Businessmen's Fellowship, called *Good News*. It came on as I was leaving the living room to check on Bonnie. I found her crying and holding some bloody tissue. Without going into the details, she'd had a spontaneous miscarriage in the few moments that I left her to make the call. We called her doctor and, by God's Grace, reached him on the first try. After hearing Bonnie's explanation of what happened, he comforted us and gave simple instructions that didn't require an immediate trip to the ER. He said to rest and be watchful for any continued loss of blood.

When I was sure Bonnie would be all right, I went back to check on Beth in the front room. When I entered I saw that the *Good News* program featured the testimony of an 11-year-old girl who had been diagnosed with an incurable form of cancer and had been miraculously healed by God. She spoke about her experience with joy, and then the program ended. As we gathered her things, Beth and I discussed the awesome story of God's love and healing power. I checked with Bonnie again, said goodbye, and we left.

In the car, I told Beth about the miscarriage and assured her Bonnie would be okay. After that, she was quiet for most of the ride home, as if deep in thought. When we were about 10 minutes from her house she asked a wonderful question.

"Dad, how do you become a Christian?"

Only God will ever know the thrill that leapt in my spirit at her words.

"Honey, you just need to ask Jesus to forgive your sins and to come into your heart to be your Lord," I said. "Do you want to be a Christian?"

"Yeah, I do, Dad."

I am not able to express what I felt at those words or explain all of the meaning and joy that they gave to me. Beth's expression of faith wasn't about me, and I had never spoken to her about the possibility of her coming to Jesus. But I had prayed for it. In fact, almost from the day that Bonnie and I were saved, and surely from the day we married, we began to pray for all the lost members in each of our families. Beth was the first on my list. Only God and Bonnie knew that.

I don't remember if I pulled off the road or waited until we got to Beth's driveway, but when the car was stopped we held hands and I was given the unspeakable privilege of helping my precious daughter ask Jesus to be her Lord and Savior. The sweetness and beauty of that moment lives in my heart. I can close my eyes to this day and see almost all of the details of that night—from Bonnie's emergency to driving back and forth from Beth's home.

I held it together pretty well while praying with Beth and assured her that God had heard her and that she was now a Christian. But when I drove away from her house I gave up all semblance of control and wept and shouted for joy! Not for me, but for Beth and for the joy of the knowledge that while I had once left her on earth and let her down, she now shared with me our Father in Heaven. A Father who would never leave her—or me—and whose love would bind us together forever. And He has.

Beth is now a beautiful, mature Christian wife and mother of two sons, whose loving walk with Jesus and faithful fruitfulness inspires me. But it hasn't been easy for her. She has been tested in many ways, and yet has stayed the course for over 40 years. Beth has taught me about grace in ways that nothing else has. I'll never stop thanking Jesus for the honor and privilege that He gave me by using me to share His redeeming love with Beth, and for His love that opened Beth's heart.

I drove home to share the joy of a new birth with Bonnie, believing it would lessen the sorrow of the birth that was not to be. I knew that I didn't "lead Beth to Christ." He did it all, but chose me as His conduit and then shared with me in the privilege and joy. Isn't that just like Him?

When Jesus saved me, I was the first and only Christian in my family that I was aware of, going as far back in our history as I could. There may have been others, but I didn't know of them. Since then, my mother, brother, sister, their spouses, and most of their children and grandchildren, have come to Christ. A little leaven does leaven the whole loaf.

Reed and His Family Meet Jesus

One of the great experiences of our company's milk route was reconnecting with my stepbrother and sister, whom I hadn't seen in over five years. Reed and Nancy Cooper had moved to Dayton, Ohio, from Iowa, and Dayton was one of the stops on my route. I got their phone number and called them during one of my first trips. They invited me to have dinner and catch up. Reed, Nancy, and their four children were a part of the family that resulted from my Dad's remarriage. We became very close initially, but had been apart for a long time due to our respective relocations.

At dinner, they were excited to hear of my time living in Rome and the great adventure that it had been. They were surprised when I told them that living and working in Italy was not the most exciting thing that happened since we last saw each other. I told them I had been born again and started a new life as a Christian. I went on to explain a few of the exciting things that had been going on in my life, and how God had moved me back to Illinois from California. They knew Bob, and were excited to hear that I worked with him in a business committed to Jesus.

Reed and Nancy were both in the workplace but had never heard of anything like what I told them. They were full of questions about what we did, the challenges we faced, and so on. We had a great discussion and when it was time to go, Reed walked me to my car.

"I'd like to know more about how to be born again," he said. "Can it happen to me?"

I told him it certainly could happen to him. Reed prayed to Jesus that night and, sure enough, it happened to him.

I called Reed a few days later at his office. He was very discouraged and said that when he told Nancy and the children he had been saved, they ridiculed him and didn't want to talk about it. We agreed to have dinner the next week, when I would be in Dayton again. I told him I would be praying for him and that he should pray for his family and trust the Lord to open their hearts.

The next week we met for dinner and afterwards went back to my hotel to pray.

Earlier that week, I read in Acts what Paul had told the Philippian jailer when he asked, "What must I do to be saved?" Paul said, "Believe on the Lord Jesus and you will be saved, you and your household." I shared the verse with Reed, and we prayed that it would be true for him as well.

Over the next few years, we met almost every week for dinner and after dinner, for prayer and Bible study in my motel room. The Lord blessed our time together and grew our faith as we shared. We saw the promises of the Word come to life before our eyes, because within two years his entire family came to Christ: first, Reed, then Nancy, and then each of their four children.

God and the Supplier

An unusual challenge came through our company's Bible study and prayer practice. We typically met as a group each morning before work, to read a chapter from Scripture and pray for the known events of the day. I attended when I was not on the milk route. One day we were reading in Romans and came across chapter 13, verse 1, that says, "Let everyone be subject to the governing authorities. For there is no authority except from God, and the authorities that exist are appointed by God" (Romans 13:1). Our habit was to alternate reading verses through a chapter and then ask ourselves, "How might that apply to what we are doing here?"

At the end of the chapter someone asked, "How does that apply to what we are doing for Toledo?" He was referring to a practice that had been in place for years: that of taking orders for liquor from our biggest customer, buying it for them in Illinois where there was no tax, and then transporting it to them across the state line, giving them a 15% tax savings. We didn't profit in the process, but it was wrong on several levels. That was clear as soon as the question left the lips of the person who asked it ... the authorities would consider us to be disobedient, illegal, and wouldn't like it a bit. But the question hung in the air.

"This is our biggest customer. What can we do?" someone asked. "If we insult them and lose their business, it would probably take us down."

It became sweaty palms time real quick. After some discussion we prayed, but came to no immediate conclusion other than we were wrong to continue to "bootleg" for the goodwill of our customer. We stewed over it for several days, when finally the Lord spoke through a member of the team.

"Just be honest. Tell them why you need to stop, and trust God."

What a concept. Be honest. Tell others why we want to honor God's Word. We determined to go to the customer to give our testimonies and explain that our business and its underlying principles had changed; we were trying to learn to follow the Bible. We would tell them we intended to live consistently with the teachings of Jesus, and that we had come to the decision that we couldn't continue some things we had done in the past. After a lot of fear and trembling, an appointment was made with the plant manager, whose name was Dave.

Three of us went to see him. We each shared how Jesus had changed our lives and that we were hoping to follow biblical principles in operating the business. Then Bob told Dave that because the Bible discouraged it, we wouldn't be able to skirt the law by bringing tax-free liquor across the state lines anymore. He said he hoped Dave would understand and that we could keep their business.

Dave looked at us with incredulity. "Do you really think that you have our business because you save us a couple of bucks on our booze?" Dave asked. "You have our business because you have the best product at the right price, and your service is very good. If and when that changes, you won't have it any longer. But until then, you have it. Now get out of here!"

He wasn't exactly smiling as he said it, but there was sort of a twinkle in his eyes. We drove home excited and celebrated God's goodness, thankful to be able to share our testimonies with Dave, and thankful for his reaction.

Experiences like those were repeated many, many times over the next 10 years I was with the company. I learned that others aren't offended when we tell them of our personal experiences, even with very personal, spiritual examples. They actually respect those who have strong beliefs. It only becomes offensive when we shake our fingers at them and preach, demanding that they believe what we believe. As long as it is our story, they can't argue with it.

There is so much pain in the world that it isn't hard to find a touch point in the lives of those around us. When we can relate our lives to what they are experiencing, it can give them encouragement and hope. Most everyone is open to that, even in the world of business. When someone would tell me about a divorce, cancer, or an addiction of a loved one, and I would offer to pray for them, their response was always, "Thank you." (I have never heard anyone say, "No, thank you.") Often, that opened the door for later opportunities when I could ask, "How is so-and-so doing?" As I grew in my faith I came to realize that the greatest thing I have to offer anyone is Jesus Christ.

The business moved me around and allowed me to meet many people … not only customers, but fellow travelers, hotel guests, and so on. I learned that the highest priority was to be sensitive to their spiritual needs and be ready to offer Jesus as their help and hope. Opportunities seldom appeared right away; they often came through the process of building a service relationship. If the pain was there, it came out. Sharing my personal faith experience at an appropriate time was the vehicle that enabled me to meet people who might never come to church or have a spiritual discussion with anyone else. God had called me to the workplace as His ambassador, and He was moving me through the world to represent Him, using my work as Vice President of Sales for the Mack Company to meet people I would never know otherwise.

That realization changed my whole perspective of the workplace. I no longer worked for a paycheck in a technical field I knew very little about and didn't really like. I realized that my work was my calling—my personal ministry—and what I did every day was eternally important. I have come to believe that I was created to do what I was learning to do then, and continue to do today … share God's love in the marketplace. I also believe that, although most don't know it, this understanding is true for every Christian in every role in life (Ephesians 4:11–12).

I believe with all my heart that the secret to joy and fulfillment in this life is to find what God has created us to do, and then to do it with all of our heart for Him. It changes everything!

Chapter 5

How God Gave Us a House When We Had No Money

We had planned to take five years to pay off our debts, but God did it somehow in two and a half. During that time, we were paying off our debts and tithing from our gross pay. We lacked nothing and God blessed us in many wonderful ways. Our two daughters, Sarah and Leah, were born healthy and beautiful. (They still are!) They were and are an ever-increasing joy in our lives. We had three vacations to visit family, and we moved from the apartment to a rented ranch-style house. And although I never spoke to Bob about my pay or even considered asking for a raise, my earnings went up and up.

After the company survived the challenge of the fire and its aftermath, God continued to show us that He wanted the business to continue. Bob and his partner reevaluated salaries and decided to put me on a commission with my small base pay restored. It wasn't much at first, but as God added business along the milk route through contacts from the Reicks organization, it grew.

The more we earned, the more we paid on our debts. And after our debts were all paid off, we continued to put the amount that we had been paying into savings instead of spending it. After a couple of years we had saved $3,500. I thought that might be enough for a down payment on a house, so we began to look around a bit. I was surprised to find that real estate had greatly appreciated since the last time I checked, and $3,500 wouldn't be enough for a down payment on a decent-sized house. At the time, we were living in a comfortable little ranch home that we rented around the corner from Bob and Holly, so there was no urgency about moving. We settled in to wait on the Lord's timing. His answer came in a very unusual way.

One morning while I was on a business trip to Texas, I called Bonnie to check on her and the girls. She didn't answer, which was unusual. I didn't think much about it and went out to make calls with our Texas rep. I called again at noon and still no answer. I began to be concerned. When I tried without success in the middle of the afternoon, I became very stressed and called the office to see if anyone had heard from Bonnie. Still nothing. Now I was frantic. When I got back to the motel to clean up before taking some customers to dinner, I called again and this time Bonnie answered.

"Where have you been?" I almost shouted. "I have been calling you all day!"

"Oh, I turned the phone ringer off when I put the girls down for their naps this morning, and forgot to turn it back on. We're fine."

Relief, mixed with another less charitable emotion, choked me.

"Well, how was your day?" I croaked.

"Sharon and Ed are going to lose their house because they are behind on their mortgage, and I was wondering if you might want to help them."

"How much do they need?" I said, still fuming inside.

"Three thousand, five hundred dollars."

"No way," I said from the depths of my charitable Christian heart. "They should have told us they were in trouble long ago, when we could have helped them with a lot less."

Sharon and Ed were part of our regular small group from church, and we had helped them out with a small loan once before. I was still so upset with Bonnie—not really with her, but with worrying about her and the girls—that I wasn't ready to do anything for anybody.

"That's okay, honey. I just thought I'd ask you," Bonnie said sweetly. "Why don't you pray about it and we can talk later?"

We chatted a few minutes and hung up.

Later I met with Jerry, a good Christian brother who was our Texas rep. As we drove for dinner I told him what had happened. We both laughed a bit, and I explained what Bonnie had asked. Jerry suggested we get together after dinner for some prayer time. We did, and it turned out to be life changing.

Back in the hotel room, Jerry suggested we look at the Scriptures for some ideas. What happened next convinced me I had been set up by God's sweet Spirit in a way that, 35 years later, is still hard to believe. I "happened" to open my Bible to the book of James and my eyes fell on the verse that read: "If a brother or sister is poorly clothed and lacking in daily food, and one of you says to them, 'Go in peace, be warmed and filled,' without giving them the things needed for the body, what good is that?" (James 2:15–16). I looked at a reference in the margin and it sent me to 1 John 3:17: "But whoever has this world's goods, and sees his brother in need and shuts his heart against him, how does the love of God abide in him?"

I got it.

Since I had an idea of how much houses cost and what it would take to get a decent home for Bonnie and the girls, I had been tempted to think about what I might do to get more money. In fact I had allowed a subtle shift from gratitude and contentment with simple provision, to thinking about getting more. God had done so much and had taken us so far in such a short time, but I was losing focus.

I shared with Jerry what I had read and what I was thinking. We prayed together and I thanked God for all He had done. Then I released all I had to Him and asked Him to show us what to do.

I slept peacefully that night, and the next morning as I stood at the sink shaving, the Holy Spirit stopped me. I began to sing a song I had never learned—at least not at any conscious level. I may have heard it somewhere but I have no recollection, and I certainly had never memorized the words.

"… Freely, freely you have received. / Freely, freely give. / Go in My name, and because you believe, / Others will know that I live."

Later I have learned that it goes on:

"All power is given in Jesus' name, / On earth and heaven, in Jesus' name. / And in Jesus' name, I come to you / To share His power as He told me to."

At that moment I knew that I knew what we were to do. I wanted to be sure that what I read the previous evening wasn't just me, so I called Bonnie. I gave her the verses and asked her to read them, and said I would call back at lunch. When I called, I asked, "What do you think they mean?"

"I think God wants us to give our money to Sharon and Ed," she immediately replied.

I agreed. "Go get a check. We'll take it over tonight."

We knocked at the door, and when Sharon opened it, we handed her the check ... folded over so the amount didn't show. "God told us to give you this," I said.

She was obviously embarrassed and didn't even look at the amount. We chatted for a few minutes and left to get back to the girls. It was perfect release. Now we had no money and no need to look for houses. It was great!

The next day the president of the local bank, who was also a member of our church, called and said that Sharon was there with the check. He asked if we wanted her to sign a note or something for the loan. I told him that it wasn't a loan, it was a gift.

"The Bible doesn't say to loan ... it says to give. The money is theirs to do with as they please," I said.

I could tell he thought that was pretty radical and probably not very smart, but he said okay and we hung up. I thought that was the end of the story, but God had more in mind. Two weeks later on a Saturday afternoon, I came in from cutting the grass and picked up the local newspaper from the front steps. I plopped down to rest a minute and, by habit, opened the paper to the "Homes for Sale" section. I wasn't looking for anything ... just scanning the section, when a very unusual offering caught my eye. "Christian family moving to Tulsa wishes to sell family home to Spirit-filled Christian family."

Huh? I had never seen anything like that before. I decided to call the number to see what was up. A young female voice answered, and I asked about the ad. She told me she was the babysitter and the owner wasn't home. But she told me about the house and described what sounded like a dream house for Bonnie and me. We both love older homes and this one had five bedrooms, an attic, basement, cut-glass windows, front porch, and so on. I asked the price and she told me.

It sounded reasonable, but when she asked if I would like to see the house, I said, "Oh no, I don't have any money. We gave our savings away and couldn't possibly afford a house now."

"Don't say that!" she admonished. "Don't you know that if God wants you to have the house, He will make a way for you to have it?"

This, from a 16-year-old! My curiosity was piqued.

"Could we come see it now?"

She said yes, so I took the address and grabbed Bonnie. After asking the neighbors to watch the girls for a few minutes, we drove to the address.

When we pulled up, Bonnie exclaimed, "I used to pass this house every day on the way to work, and I loved the porch and the lilac trees in front. I often thought what a great house it would be for a family."

We met the girl at the door and she showed us the house. It was 10 times what we would have hoped to have. It was a real old beauty with high ceilings, hardwood floors, and tons of room—way more than we would ever need. The price was reasonable, but way beyond our means, of course. The girl said the owner wanted to go to Bible school in Tulsa and was believing God would sell the house in time for the fall semester. It was now August.

"In fact," she said, "the owner is having a garage sale tomorrow to begin to get ready to go."

We said that we might come by and meet her, and then left. Bonnie and I sat in the car for a few minutes, looking at the house in rueful amusement. We had no money and no hope of getting any, yet there sat our dream house. We prayed.

"Lord, thank You for all You have done to bring us to this time. We love this house, but only want it if it is Your will. Of course You know that You will have to provide all the money somehow, but more than that, if it is Your will that we have it, we ask You to have the owner say so. We'll leave it with You, Father, in Jesus' name."

We drove home. After we picked up the girls and were walking into the house, the phone rang. It was Sharon.

"We want to thank you for the money you gave us, but we don't need it anymore. We want to give it all back."

"Sharon," I said, "it wasn't a loan and we don't expect you to give it back. It's yours."

"No," she said, "we used it to have our house appraised, and it's worth much more than what we paid for it. So we were able to refinance and get a new mortgage, and a bit extra." She sounded happy. "We don't need the money and want to return it. It's like you loaned us your lawn mower and we're done with it. We'll bring you a check to church tomorrow."

I sat down and shared the news with Bonnie. The money wasn't near enough for a down payment on the house we just saw, but it was more money than we had a few minutes before. We had a strange excitement that something was up.

After church the next day, we returned to the house and met Jane, the owner. She was indeed having a garage sale in anticipation of moving to Oklahoma. We looked around while she waited on some customers. When she had a break, we sat with her in the living room and shared our testimonies. As we did, a couple of her friends came in. One of them sat at the piano and began to play hymns softly. In a minute we were all singing and praising the Lord. It was a spontaneous prayer-and-praise meeting among brothers and sisters who, only minutes ago, were strangers. It was a wonderful Spirit-led experience.

I told Jane our story of giving all of our savings away at God's direction, how they had returned the money the night before, and that there was nothing we could do to raise more money. I said I understood that we would not be able to buy the house unless God performed a miracle, and if someone else came along and bought it in the meantime, we would know it wasn't for us. I told her if that happened, we would be fine, and would pray for her and her need to get to Tulsa in a month. We left their house blessed and at peace. Just having the chance to see the house and imagine what might be one day, and to meet and pray and worship with the neat new friends was such a true "serendipity in Jesus."

The next day, Monday, I was in town working at my desk when Bonnie called.

"You'll never guess what just happened," she said excitedly. "Jane called and said that she and her friends continued in prayer after we left, and one of them told her they felt God was saying it was His will that we have the house." She paused to catch her breath. "She said she agreed and she would give us a contract to rent/purchase, with all of our payments credited towards the equity we need to get a conventional mortgage." She laughed and said, "Can you believe it? She said we could move in three weeks!"

I was stunned. How could it be? On Saturday afternoon I had no money and no thought of buying a home for several years to come. On Monday, without any effort, striving, or manipulation on my part, I was about to not only buy a house, but buy a house beyond my wildest dreams. I called Jane. She confirmed it and we discussed how it would work. I still have a copy of the ad I saw and the simple, one-page agreement that we signed committing as brother and sister in Jesus, to honor our word and complete the contract to honor God. And that is what we did.

Bonnie and I loved that house. We didn't love it because it was a great house, we loved it for what it stood for in God. We knew without a doubt He gave it to us, and we knew He must have plans for us to use it in the Kingdom somehow. Throughout the eight years we lived there, we were able to share it with numerous Christians who had need of a place to stay for a variety of reasons. Some to attend Bible school, others attempting to reconcile marriage, and Bonnie's younger brother who needed a home away from home. We welcomed all of them to come live with us. It was an anointed home, and we still remember the thrill of the memory of God's sovereign provision.

***

As part of Jesus' teaching process, we were involved in a wonderful small gathering called a Koinoinia group. It was the same one that Sharon and Ed were part of, with about six or seven couples from our church. It was exciting to be with others who were about where we were in their faith experience, and learn together about things like prayer and faith.

Most of us had never prayed out loud in public, when we started to study a book titled *The Edge of Adventure*. The book was written for new Christians, and over the course of a year it led us through most of the basics of Christian life. When we finished, we studied another book about the person of the Holy Spirit. One of the gals in the group "happened" to have it in her purse when the subject of what to do after we finished the first book came up. We grew closer as a group and in our faith as well.

The book, *The Holy Spirit and You: A Guide to the Spirit-Filled Life*, by Dennis and Rita Bennett, taught us that the work of the Holy Spirit goes on today and still does what Jesus did when He was here physically. It addressed things like healing, and dealing with evil spirits ... topics we had never considered. We approached the subjects slowly and tried to listen for His voice, and then we experimented with what we learned.

One of the couples had a son who had developed a serious enlargement of his spleen. He was very sick and the doctors scheduled surgery to remove it. We were at his parents' home, meeting with our group sitting around their dining room table, when I noticed a weird-looking fresco hanging on the wall. I asked what it was and was told it was the signs of the zodiac. We had studied how evil spirits can attach themselves to idols and that astrology is a form of witchcraft. I asked more about it and was told the fresco had been purchased at a garage sale.

As we looked at it and discussed what it stood for, I thought the Lord spoke into my spirit: *Smash the fresco and I will set the boy free.* I had read in the Bible about the Christian people of Ephesus smashing pagan idols and burning their scrolls (Acts 19), but I was hesitant to speak. I had no idea what the thing was worth or how the hosts would respond. But the sense that I should speak out and trust God was strong. I finally spoke up.

"Sharon, I think God said that if you will smash the fresco, He will heal Scott. Astrology is a form of witchcraft."

The words were hardly out of my mouth before the husband handed me a hammer. We went into the backyard and prayed to Jesus, rejecting the spirit of astrology and every form of idolatry and witchcraft. Then we smashed the thing to pieces. We all felt an excitement about what we had done and sensed that something good had happened. That was Friday. On Monday, Scott went in for a pre-op checkup. His spleen and blood counts were normal.

Once, the husband of a couple we knew was diagnosed with a brain tumor and he was in the hospital. We laid our hands on his wife in his place and asked Jesus to heal him. He left the hospital a few days later, healed without further treatment.

Another time, one of the wives in our group developed a problem that was going to require a hysterectomy. She didn't want that since the couple still wanted children. We prayed and prayed for her, but the problem persisted and surgery was scheduled.

The night before surgery I was away on a trip, reading my Bible and praying in my room. I read the passage in Isaiah where God says, "Is my arm so short that it cannot save?" (Isaiah 59:1). As I mulled it over, the thought came to me to call my friend and reassure her. When she answered I told her not to give up or lose faith, that if it was God's will that she have more children He would make a way, and to just rest in Him. She thanked me and we had a short prayer.

The next morning she was prepped for surgery and wheeled into the operating room. While she was in the dreamy pre-op state, her neighbor, who happened to be the hospital's chief anesthesiologist, stopped by her gurney. He said he was surprised to see her. While he was speaking, she tried to blow some stray hair out of her face because she couldn't move her arms. As she puffed at the stray hair, he reached over to brush it back.

"Pat, you have a fever," he said. "Nurse, take this patient's temperature."

The nurse did, and Pat had a 101-degree fever. Just then, her surgeon came into the OR.

"What's the problem?" he asked.

When the doctor was told of the fever, he said it was no problem and he intended to proceed with the surgery.

"Not on your life," said the anesthesiologist. "There will be no surgery on a patient running a fever."

The doctors disputed for a few minutes before the hospital's chief anesthesiologist pulled rank. He said that no anesthesiologist would be allowed to serve under those conditions. Pat was returned to her room.

When she came out of the haze of the pre-op, she and her husband had a talk and decided to put off surgery indefinitely. The husband later started to do some investigation of the doctor and found that he was the subject of a number of malpractice lawsuits and had received numerous complaints. What her husband learned convinced them to get another opinion. The new doctor they visited found that Pat was diabetic and that was the cause of her problem. If the operation had gone forward, it was possible she could have bled to death.

After a few months of treatment, Pat conceived and delivered a healthy baby girl. The Lord's arm is not short, and I wonder how that chief anesthesiologist "happened" to stop by at that time? Hmmmm.

Of course, healing didn't happen that way every time. We learned that God is sovereign and He knows what is best. Sometimes He is working in ways we can't see or know, and His answers come in far different ways. Still, it was such a powerful time, and God continues to work.

Chapter 6

New Direction

The Mack Company was growing nicely after the traumatic first couple of years. One day, Bob received an interesting phone call from a company that was a big player in the automotive parts manufacturing space—our sweet spot and focus. They were a supplier of a related product that, when used in conjunction with our synthetic coolant, experienced significantly improved performance.

The chairman of the company was calling to ask if we would be willing to sell the business to him. Under many circumstances, that would be a tempting—even flattering—offer. But in our case, we quickly recognized that such a sale would severely limit, if not end, our ability to operate the business as if Jesus were the owner. The other company was not known as an evil business per se, but as a typical tough competitor with a worldly orientation.

We prayed about how to respond. We didn't want to offend the chairman, but were determined we couldn't go forward to explore the offer. We decided to ask the chairman for a meeting with the purpose of sharing our testimonies and our experiences with our business to date.

The Lord prompted us to share first, and if the chairman seemed willing to discuss our perspective and was open to an alternative, we would offer a private label deal. Such an arrangement would essentially give them access to our products and guarantee our ability to supply them, or give access to our formulas to be produced elsewhere.

Needless to say, we were apprehensive when the three of us sat down with the chairman. We each shared our testimony and briefly told him about our having committed the business to Christ. We expressed our desire to be able to see any kind of business arrangement through while keeping our independence. He listened attentively.

When we had finished, he looked at us, not unkindly, and said, "I don't share you boys' religious enthusiasm, but I understand your desire to see your dream through. In fact, that's why I have never sold this business ... I wanted to be free to call my own shots. Is there some way we could work together?"

With great relief we suggested a private label alternative and he immediately saw the win-win possibilities in it. He said it would be a great arrangement. We would package the product in his containers and offer him access to the formulation if we were unable to supply his need. We had a few more minutes of pleasant conversation and discussed some of the basic outlines of the private label supply contract. Then the interview was over.

On the way out, the chairman asked if we would like to have a plant tour, and we jumped at the chance. Near the end of the tour he took us into the R&D lab. When we walked through, Bob noticed a funny-looking contraption off to one side and asked about it.

"Oh, that's an experimental filter we're working on for some folks who want to develop a synthetic lubricant for making two-piece aluminum cans. Have you ever thought of that? You seem to have some interesting synthetic technology."

"What are two-piece cans?" Bob asked. We had never heard the term and had no idea what it meant.

"That's the latest thing in beer and beverage cans. Instead of a top, a bottom, and a rolled steel can with a welded side seam, they're trying to produce aluminum in the shape of a can and put a top on the formed body. That's why they call them two-piece cans—the old style is called three-piece. There are two companies working hard on this concept right now, and you should talk to them. One is in Chicago and the other in Denver. I'll give you their names if you like."

Of course we liked! Bob's gift was inventing new lubricants, and we explored any and all applications we found. We left the meeting rejoicing at God's goodness. We had been very concerned about discussing our desire to be a Christian witness with this powerful man, but not only had he been gracious to hear us out, he seemed friendly and wanted to help us. The door was open for a relationship, and who knew where it might lead?

Over the next few days, we contacted both of the companies the chairman told us about and were well received. Indeed, they were actively researching the area of synthetic lubricants and would be happy to receive our samples. We chose to work first with the closest, a huge can manufacturer located in Chicago.

Since I was available on the day the sample was ready, I took it into the prospect's lab and actually saw two-piece cans being made on a laboratory machine. It was fascinating. These machines, I learned, would produce at a rate of 60–90 strokes per minute ... each stroke stretching a piece of aluminum into the shape of a can. The test machine was a bit slow, as designed, but still very impressive. I couldn't wait to get back and report what I saw.

I also heard a brief explanation of the developing market for a successful synthetic lubricant. It was huge and still growing. Whoever developed a successful product would get a ton of business. The push for environmentally compatible products was just beginning, and the oil-based products used at the time would soon be unacceptable because of the contaminated wastewater in the cleaning process. The problem was that all of the lubricant had to be cleaned from the formed can's surface before the coating and printing could be applied.

Back at the office, we went to work researching beverage can producers. We learned there were only about 85 locations in the world that produced two-piece cans, and most of them intended to change from tin to aluminum production for a variety of reasons. What a wonderful scenario for a small business with a very limited budget! In an hour we located every possible customer in the world and their corporate and/or R&D locations. If we could build a successful product, we could compete with much larger businesses in a way we never could in a broader, less defined market. Even with our limited resources we were extremely excited to imagine what could happen.

Of course there was the thing about having a *potentially* successful product, so we waited for the results of our product's trial that was scheduled for the following week. And what about our competitors? We were going head-to-head with enormous companies like Amoco, Shell, Cincinnati-Milicron, Nalco, Texaco, and others. Those guys spilled more than we produced! But the Lord had a plan. The next week we were told that we had been selected to enter into a joint development agreement to produce the product. God's provision was truly amazing.

We decided I should not take my eye off the milk route that produced about a third of our revenues by that time. We would assign someone else to pursue what we were now calling the new "can lube" market. That was fine with me, since I really enjoyed the fellowship of the Reicks guys and the other customers that the Lord was providing. In an amazingly short period of time, this small group (among whom I was the supposed expert) received orders from GM, International Harvester, Chrysler, and other giant companies—often right out from under much larger and better-equipped competitors.

I saw a pattern develop that God has used with me over and again. He would put me in a situation where I knew I was over my head and couldn't do what was needed to be done to succeed. And then when success happened, I couldn't miss seeing it was His doing and not mine. This has been His way with me to this day. I am thick and slow, but even I couldn't fail to see His hand in what was happening.

The field trial of the can lube was successful and we waited for the first order for a longer production trial. Although we started with great anticipation, for some reason things stalled and were going nowhere. After several months we approached our development partners and asked to negotiate independent sales rights to the product whereby we would pay them a royalty on sales. Surprisingly, they agreed.

The next big problem was that it was terribly difficult to get a production trial. It was a significant risk for the producer to gamble on an unknown product since a typical can manufacturing plant made one million cans per day minimum, and any disruption of production could be very costly. We were not having much success landing the first major commitment. People were glad to talk with us, but the end of the conversation was typically, "Call us when you have a customer we can talk to." It was frustrating, especially for Bob.

One day I "happened" to be in Cincinnati when I stopped for a break and called the office to talk to Bob. After we got caught up on the week's events, he asked if I had a data sheet on the can lube product. I "happened" to have one. Although I wasn't involved with the sale, I had helped write the data sheet and kept a copy. Bob asked if I would mind making a detour to call on a small can manufacturer that he heard of in one of the suburbs of Cincinnati.

"No problem," I said. "Who should I call on?"

"Ask for Tom Brown ... he's the chemical engineer," Bob said.

I hung up and called the number Bob had given me. A man answered and I asked for Tom Brown.

"Tom's on vacation this week. Can I help you?" the pleasant voice asked. "What do you need?"

I explained that we had developed a new synthetic product and that I just wanted to drop off a data sheet.

"C'mon over, I'll take it," said Paul Smith. "I'm the mechanical guy, but I'll give it to Tom when he comes back."

I got directions and drove to the plant.

Paul greeted me and took me back to his office. He was a great guy and we hit it off right away ... another one of those *coincidental* things. While we were still talking (not about can lube, but getting to know each other), in walked another man who Paul introduced as Frank, the plant manager. I didn't fully appreciate it at the time, but later understood that not just anybody gets to meet the plant manager in a can making plant. But there I was with Frank and, again, meeting another great guy about my age, and from the Chicago area who also loved to play golf. Frank asked why I was there. I told him about our R&D project and our products, and that we were looking for a trial. You could have knocked me over with a feather when Frank spoke up.

"Oh, well, we're going to start a series of trials next week. Can you be ready to run then?"

"Of course," I said, not having a clue how we would do it. I was so excited by the prospect that I didn't know what else to say. Remember, I was in sales.

"Fine," said Frank, "let's do it. I'll see you then."

After Paul and I visited a few minutes more, I left.

Bursting with excitement, I called Bob and he was blown away as well. Surely, this was God at work, but we had no idea how this new opportunity would lead us to places we had never imagined.

Because I was the one who had started the relationship, it was decided that I should go along for the trial. Bob got all the product and gear together in record time, and the next Monday we found ourselves in a real can plant trial. By that time, Tom had come back from vacation and Paul had briefed him. He turned us over to Tom for the trial. We got an early start and the test was humming along.

At about lunchtime, Frank, the plant manager, walked up. "How's it going?" he asked.

We all said it was looking good, and then Paul approached us from the other direction.

"How about lunch?" Frank asked. "Do you like cheeseburgers?" (Truly a man after my own heart.)

The five of us went to lunch and the burgers were great. When we returned to the factory and checked to see that the test was still going well, Paul tapped me on the shoulder and asked me to step out to the loading dock. It is extremely noisy in a can plant and difficult to converse beyond one-word sentences and sign language. Outside, Paul asked me if he could ask me a personal question. I said sure.

"I noticed that you and Bob both bowed your heads before you ate at lunch. Were you saying grace?"

"Yes," I said, "we always give the Lord thanks for our food."

"What religion are you?"

"I'm a Christian."

"I mean, are you a Catholic or a Baptist, or what?"

"No, I'm just a Christian."

"What does that mean?"

"It means I believe in Jesus and I'm trying to learn to follow Him."

"I've never heard of that. Would you be willing to come to my house and tell my wife and me what you mean?"

You know where this is going. Paul and his wife, Jan, and I had dinner that night and I shared my testimony with them. By "coincidence," the movie *The Hiding Place* was playing in the theater nearby. I asked them if they would like to go and learn some more. The movie was about a Dutch family who protected some Jews from the Nazis during World War II, and how their faith both cost them and helped them. I had only read about the movie, but it seemed a great bridge for the topic of the evening.

We were all brought to tears as we watched Corrie ten Boom and her sister endure suffering in a Nazi concentration camp while maintaining their faith. They even had joy in Jesus under circumstances that one could not imagine. At the end of the movie an invitation to receive Christ was given, and Paul and Janet both received the gift of salvation. It was quite a day.

Looking back, how evident it is that God was in it all. I happened to be in Cincinnati. Paul happened to answer Tom's phone. Frank happened to walk into the office and then come by at lunch. What I didn't know then was that Paul and Janet had been talking to a divorce lawyer the week before, and Paul had visited the Jehovah's Witness church the previous two weekends. Just coincidence? Twenty-four members of their family have come to Christ as a direct result of their witness. Just coincidence? You'll never convince me so.

That's what is so important about this period. Such lessons and arrangements from God are eternal and He used them and many more in the years that followed, to show me how business is truly a vehicle for Christ.

Chapter 7

Miracles of Provision in the Business

One day I was on a service call at Heekin Can, checking on the performance of our product. We had moved from being used in one trial machine, on into their central system, and were now supplying the whole production line. I was checking the line when two men in suits came by. They were obviously from outside of the company, and they were carefully observing the whole production process. They asked who I was and why I was there. When I told them I was from the supplier of the new synthetic lubricant, they were all ears.

It turned out that one of them was Bob Jones, plant manager of Pearl Container in San Antonio, Texas. The other was Doug Law from Miller Container in Ft. Worth. I have already mentioned how hard it was to get to see the manager of a can plant, but here were two great prospects asking great questions, who saw the good performance of our innovative product with their own eyes.

This was another example of how God has done things in a way that I couldn't take credit for. I was still on my milk route and only "happened" to be in Cincinnati as part of my four-city trip. It made sense that I would keep the primary contact at Heekin because of our existing relationship, but my primary responsibility was still with our industrial product line and the milk route. When I planned my visit to Heekin, it was logically the best time to be there. I had no idea that I would see anyone but my usual contact, or do anything beyond saying "Hello" and "Can I do anything for you?"

We kept close contact with our clients by phone as part of normal service, and my presence was just part of the strategy of customer service that we had adopted. We intended to make all our customers feel as if we were "local." But meeting the men from Pearl Container was clearly a divine appointment which led to our big break into the high-volume can lube business. First we were given the opportunity to serve Pearl and then, a bit later, Miller Container in Ft. Worth. They gave us entrée into their six plants and, because they had an agreement with Reynolds Aluminum, into their 10 or so additional plants.

We were doubly blessed with the Pearl Container account. Through a friendly relationship with an ink vendor that we met while servicing the Pearl plant, we were introduced to Lone Star Container—another local San Antonio brewer who manufactured their own cans. And then through them, we met American Can Company's technical advisors and gained entrée to their multiple plants.

All of these encounters that became substantial business were the result of our going to tell a powerful man that we couldn't sell the company to him. Instead, we shared our testimony of how Jesus had changed our lives and how we wanted to learn His ways in business. It all came from "happening" to be in Cincinnati on the milk route on a day when Paul would take Ron's call and Frank would walk into Paul's office during the 15-minute window when I would be there … and so on. You get the picture? No one would be so foolish as to claim credit for all the providential situations that led to our becoming the first and largest supplier of synthetic process lubricants to the two-piece can industry in the world within five years.

***

The can lube business growth had stretched our company in every way you can imagine. Eventually we had to choose to let go of the industrial product sales work to service the can business. One of the main problems facing a fast-growing business is cash flow—generating and collecting enough money to pay for the increased costs of production as sales increased. Many businesses fail for this reason: their inability to manage net cash flow during fast growth. We were in a very tight spot and though we were selling more each month, we couldn't deliver the product and collect the money fast enough to pay our suppliers on time. We had to juggle the payments as best we could, but were still falling behind.

One of our biggest suppliers was a large multinational business with a specialty chemicals division. The general manager, a man named Hugh, was intrigued by our increasing purchases of one of their new products, and he visited us to find out what we were using it for and to develop a relationship. He and Bob hit it off quickly, and Bob shared our mission statement with him: "This business exists to bring honor and glory to God, and to do business in a way that will allow His Son, Jesus, to say, 'Well done, good and faithful servants.' "

Hugh was intrigued, since he had never seen a company integrate faith in their business model before. While not a practicing believer, Hugh was a God-fearing man. He stayed the whole day and although he didn't know it at the time, God was using him to provide the key element in our ability to manage our growth.

Hugh asked Bob how his company could help us. In his inspired, half-serious reply, Bob asked Hugh if it were possible for them to give us 90-day credit terms. Normal credit terms were 30 days and we couldn't possibly order the raw materials, blend our formulation, package it, ship it, and receive payment—all within 30 days. This was the heart of the cash-flow problem. If our supplier would extend the requirement to pay for the products we ordered to 90 days, we would have plenty of time to handle the increasing volume.

Hugh said that they would do it if they could add a percent or two to our cost to offset their cost of money. Bob easily agreed. That was the start of another example of God's provision for the growth of our company, and would eventually enable us to be sent out much farther as ambassadors for Christ. Almost overnight, our business changed from a primarily local business operating in the Midwest, to a global supplier of a niche product. It also allowed us to grow at a 15–40% rate and pay our bills on time. That one encounter paved the way for our revenues to grow tenfold over the next seven years.

Bob approached our other suppliers with the same request and they all agreed, including another key vendor owned by a Jewish man. In reality, without this extended payment provision across the board, we would have been required to sell the business or go bankrupt. It would have been another classic form of rapid growth leading to insolvency.

God's provision through Hugh was critical and essential, but it was not something that we had devised or planned. It came almost jokingly, as part of a friendly conversation with a man who was a stranger and who became a dear friend. Hugh ended up renewing his commitment to Jesus through the relationship with Bob and our company.

***

God's provision doesn't always come in ways that we recognize immediately. Sometimes it comes in the form of challenges or disguised as a trial. An example of this principle would begin to unfold in the form of a lawsuit against us by a customer and development partner.

The fact that we were served papers citing us as having illegally stolen proprietary information from our partner was one of the greatest shocks I have ever experienced. It was shocking in that our development agreement with the other company specifically stated that we would bring chemical expertise to the partnership, and that we would jointly develop a product that would be for the partner's use. We later negotiated the rights to sell it to others. The suit claimed that we had stolen knowledge of a component chemical that was proprietary to our partner, when in actuality the chemical was produced by a third party and advertised for use in our application. The component was clearly described in a publicly distributed piece of literature. The suit made no sense.

When we consulted an attorney, he suggested we counter-sue for slander and harassment, commenting that he had never seen such a blatant error in judgment. He urged us to file a claim against our partner.

We had no idea what was behind the action, but we learned a principle that was helpful when trying to understand problems that don't make sense: "When something doesn't make sense in the natural, look for the supernatural." The lawsuit didn't make any sense, so we turned to Jesus. "Lord, what is this and what should we do?" We prayed for two weeks, but heard nothing.

Sometime later, I was on a business trip in Scotland and called Bob at the end of the day, as usual.

"I think I know what we are to do about the suit," Bob said after we had chatted briefly.

"What?" I asked.

"Do you have your Bible handy?"

I said I did.

"Look up Matthew 5:40."

I got my Bible and read, "If anyone wants to sue you and take away your tunic, let him have your cloak also."

"What do you think that means for us?" I asked.

"I think I should ask to speak to the court and tell them we are a Christian company learning to apply the Bible in our business. I'll read the Matthew Scriptures to them and tell them that based on what it says, while we don't acknowledge any guilt at all, we will pay them whatever they ask."

"But Bob, they could put us out of business!" I gasped.

"If this is really the Lord's business, He will protect us. Pray about it tonight and call me in the morning."

I went to prayer with my Bible open in front of me. As I read and reread the words of Jesus, His peace came to me and I sensed an agreement with Bob that this was exactly what we should do. I called Bob the next morning and told him. We prayed together and that afternoon he followed through. He asked the judge for permission, read the verse, and offered to pay whatever our partner asked.

The judge acknowledged that while this was highly unusual, he said it was legal and asked the partner what they wanted. The partners were so surprised that they said they didn't know, and asked for 24 hours to consider. They came back the next day and told the court that they wanted $250,000. Of course we didn't have that amount or anything close to it, but that was when we saw God's hand move. The partners asked for payment as an override on the sales of products containing the disputed chemical for the next five years, with a balloon payment of any balance due at the end. Bob agreed.

When I called later, he told me about all that had happened. It was an unjust suit because we hadn't done what we were accused of doing. Our response made no sense in worldly terms, but we had done what we felt was God's will and had released the situation to Him.

Over the next two years our sales rose dramatically. In the second year we had a $1 million pretax profit. We had never before had a profit anywhere near that. We paid off the judgment two and a half years early and moved on. But we never learned the true reason for the suit.

I'm not saying that every Christian, or every Christian business, should do what we did. Nor am I saying the result of what happened was that we grew fast and experienced a huge profit. You decide for yourself. There is no "cause and effect" way to put God in a box. But I do believe that God honors those who honor Him, and that as we try to obey His Word and do what it says—even when we err on the side of obedience—His Grace can cover us in a way that nothing else can.

***

The business continued to expand, and soon we were in need of a representative in Texas. So God led us to an unusual hire ... a young man we knew from Texas who headed a Christian ministry in Aurora, Illinois.

One day Bob asked me, "What would you think about talking to Jerry about the job?"

Strangely, I'd also had that thought, but didn't think Jerry would leave what he was doing. I agreed, saying, "What can we lose by asking?"

We talked to Jerry that day. Needless to say, we were surprised when he told us he and his wife had been praying about a move back to Texas because they wanted to be near their aging parents. He said they would pray about it, and after a few days we came to an agreement. It was a bit risky because Jerry had no prior sales experience, and Texas was fast becoming our best territory. But we felt that a man who could lead kids in street evangelism would have no fear, and would represent the Lord extremely well. In about two months, Jerry and his wife found a good deal on a house in their hometown, bought it with their first paycheck as a down payment, and got to work.

During his third week on the job, Jerry was making a sales call on a customer in Oklahoma and mentioned the new house. The client asked him if he had purchased mortgage insurance, and Jerry said he hadn't. The man said he was a part-time agent, and asked if Jerry would be interested in having a policy. Jerry agreed. They made a deal and the man made an appointment for Jerry to have a routine physical exam. The policy was not very large, and the exam should have been almost perfunctory, but it turned out to be extremely providential.

As Jerry lay on his back, the doctor felt his stomach and noticed something. He ordered Jerry to the hospital for an X-ray. When it was developed, it revealed a large tumor. Jerry had been in perfect health, as far as he knew, and had no clue that anything was wrong. The doctor ordered surgery and it was scheduled quickly. What should have been a one-hour procedure in fact took six. It turned out to be a complex tumor that the doctor said could have been fatal if left untended, even for a couple more weeks, since it had wound itself around the intestine. We prayed with Jerry on the phone the day after the operation, and he said that he instantly felt the pain diminish. Jerry's voice gained noticeable strength as we talked and prayed. The healing had truly begun as we prayed.

Think about it. If Bob hadn't listened to God, or if we hadn't been willing to be radical in hiring an accountant/minister to steward our best territory, and if Jerry hadn't bought the house to go to work with us and called on our customer, he would very likely have died. We and the world would have lost a great servant of Christ.

Jerry went on to be our very best sales rep and was a cornerstone to the ministry in, and through, the business.

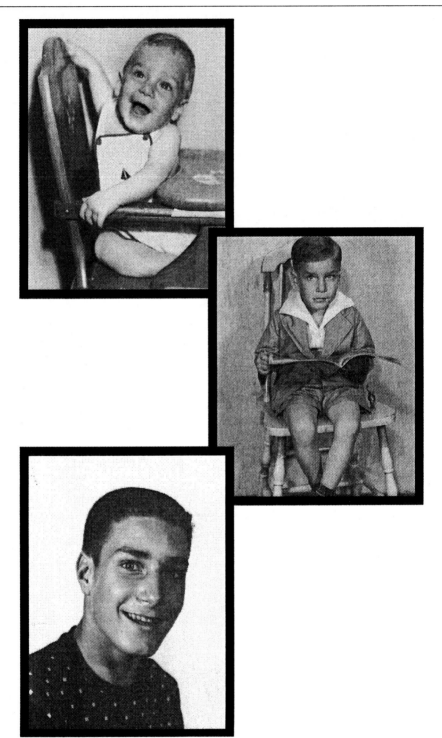

The Italian Villa

Buck & Bonnie—1979

Wedding Day

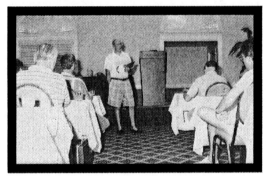

Early FCCI Training

The substance of this Agreement which is entered
into with both parties asking our Lord's blessing and believing
in His Commandments regarding the conduct of our lives, and
trusting that it is His will that this Agreement be made, is
that insofar as it is under my control, I will do nothing to
harm the interest of Jane K. Eshagpoor in this house and will
with every effort try to enhance it. In return, I ask no more
than the same. It is my wish that our common bond of the love
of Jesus, who is the living Christ, will be far more important
in the execution of this sale than any earthly contract. On
this basis, I sign my name.

LAW OFFICE OF
WILTON CASTRO
125 NORTH LAKE STREET
AURORA, ILLINOIS 60906
(312) 859-0122

The Agreement for the House God Gave Us

The House that God Gave Us

A Chair Training Session

Don, Buck & Troy

Bob & Holly Mack

+LDM   11th July, '97
Dear Friends (The C-12 Group),
        God loves you for the love you
give and the joy you share through
your gift for our Poor. It will
enable us bring Hope into the lives
of many in despair, helping them once
again experience that Divine love to
which we are all called to share.

        Keep the joy of being loved by
God ever burning in your heart as
your strength and share it with all
you meet by your thoughtful love and
humble service.

                    GOD BLESS YOU,

                    Ac Teresa mc

God bless you
Ac Teresa mc

Buck's 70th Birthday

Buck & Bob at the Mack Company

Buck & Bonnie at Communion

Chairs Sharing Communion

Chapter 8

Ted's Story

As I traveled in my role as VP of Sales, God made it clear that business was a great vehicle for sharing His love and His way of life with others. One of the most amazing experiences I had took me back to where it all started … Los Angeles, California, and Ted Brooks.

The can lube business had continued to grow and when we gained a can plant account in the Los Angeles area, I was sent to make a call to explore other opportunities there. Almost immediately I called Ted, and he invited me to have dinner with him and his wife, Liz. They had opened a bakery south of the UCLA campus. We met there before going to their house.

We'd had little contact in the years since I left LA, and Ted was eager to hear all that had happened in my faith journey. He shook his head in amazement as I described the way God had taken us through the refining fire of various tests and trials. I told him about the growth of the company and the excitement I had for a business that could both serve the Lord and grow as a result of applying best business practices based on God's Word. Our conversation ranged widely as I explained many answers to prayers, such as how God pulled Bonnie and me out of debt even while we were giving the first tenth away, and how blessed we had been since giving our hearts to Jesus.

After dinner, Ted asked a wonderful question.

"Buck, is this just something that God has for you, or can anyone know Him this way?"

Of course I told him I was nobody special and that God's love and relationship was for him also, if he would accept God's gift of forgiveness and salvation in Jesus.

"Can I have it?" he asked.

You know the rest. The man who first told me I needed God didn't really know Him, and God used me to introduce them. It was a great thrill and I realized it was a special blessing. But I had no idea how the ripples would spread from that moment on. His wife, Liz, also accepted Jesus. The Butterfly Bakery became a mission outpost where the homeless and hungry were fed, and where Ted would "hold court," sitting at a round table and engaging the flow of people who came by. Before I left, he said he wanted me to meet someone on my next trip to LA.

When I returned a couple weeks later, Ted invited me to dinner again (it became a regular event on my business visits to the area). He introduced me to one of his clients, a singer who was the younger daughter of a famous singer I knew to be Jewish. I don't have permission to use their last names, but the younger sister's name is Roz. When I arrived at Ted's apartment, Roz was already there.

"Buck," he said, "this is Roz and she needs to know Jesus." And then he turned to her. "Roz, you need to listen to Buck."

I was completely embarrassed, and Roz blushed as well. I'd grown to love Ted and his direct, sometimes abrasive manner, but I wasn't ready for this. Still, I was surprised at the words that came out of my mouth. I had never spoken of Jesus to a Jew before and I knew it could be very delicate.

"Roz, do you believe in God?" I asked.

"Of course I do," she answered.

"Do you believe He answers prayer?"

"I do," she replied.

"Well, if Jesus is truly the Messiah, wouldn't you like to know it?"

"I would."

"Well, then, why don't you ask God?"

"I will."

"That's great!" I said. Then I turned to Ted. "What's for dinner?"

We quickly moved on to talk about other things. Roz was a sweet person and fun to be with. She was trying hard to get started in the music business, but was having a tough time. The rest of the evening was pleasant, and then we wrapped it up. I left without any further discussion about God.

Two weeks later, on my next trip, I went to Ted's for dinner again and Roz was there as well. She was sort of glowing. I couldn't speak to her at dinner because there were other guests who were Jewish and I didn't want to embarrass anyone. But after dinner I found myself sitting on the couch with Roz while the others were occupied.

"Roz, you look different tonight. Has something good happened for you?" I asked.

"Yes," she replied with a big smile.

"You've asked Jesus into your heart, haven't you?"

"Yes, I did," she said, grinning. "I asked God, like you said, and He told me Jesus was my Savior. So I asked Him, and He answered!"

What a concept ... just ask God!

We didn't have any more private moments that night, but sometime later I was blessed to be invited to watch Roz make her first record. The Bible that I had given to Ted, and which he had given to her, was on the music stand with her. Of course I replaced it with another Bible for Ted. He had become a lightning rod for Jesus.

A few months later when I called to tell Ted I was in town, he asked me if I could come to dinner. I said I could, and he asked if I would mind if a neighbor joined us.

"He is really down," he said, "and he has just been diagnosed with throat cancer."

"Maybe we can cheer him up with some good news," I said.

"You better be careful what you say. He's Jewish and doesn't want to hear about Jesus."

I told him that was fine and I would just try to be encouraging for the man who turned out to be named Joe Wolf. We ate a cordial dinner, and a lot of the conversation focused on the business and how we were seeing God's hand in and through it. I was able to gently explain how Ted had helped me find the Lord.

"That's wonderful," Joe said. "Of course I am a Jew and we only believe in the Old Testament."

"I'm a Jew too," I said, "through adoption. Did you know there are well over a hundred prophesies in the Old Testament that identify Jesus as the Messiah?"

Joe said he didn't know that. The warmth in his response led me to ask if he would like to see some of the prophesies. He immediately said he would, and we got up and moved to the couch where Ted kept an ornate family Bible. I showed Joe Isaiah 53. As we read this and a couple of other verses, the light came on in Joe's eyes.

So I asked the question: "Joe, would you like to receive the sacrifice that Jesus made for your sins and ask Him to save you, like He has Ted and me?"

"I sure would!" Joe replied.

We prayed together, with me leading and Joe following, in the "Sinner's Prayer." As we were closing, I began to pray for Joe's throat cancer.

He put his hand gently on my arm and stopped me. "God's done quite enough for me for one night," he said.

I knew then that his prayer was sincere. He wasn't asking God to heal him in his body—maybe later. But Joe understood what God had done for his soul, and he wanted to soak that in. Joe was a sweet man, and we developed a friendship that only lasted a few years, until God brought Joe home and healed him forever. But until then, we often prayed together on the phone or whenever I was in town. I truly look forward to seeing Joe again.

"God's done quite enough," he'd said. Indeed He had.

***

Another Ted Story

I was at home in Illinois one evening and Ted called.

"Buck, you have to call a friend of mine. He is in a motel on Cape Cod and says he is going to commit suicide. I told him you were the only one who can help, and you've got to call him now."

"Ted, I don't know how to help him. What can I do?"

"Tell him about Jesus … that's what he needs."

I argued a bit, but Ted was adamant. I finally agreed. I was about to call the number he gave me but before I did, Bonnie and I prayed together for the man whose name was John. We opened the Bible for guidance, and my gaze fell on John 3:35–36: "The Father loves the Son and has placed everything in His hands. Whoever believes in the Son has eternal life."

I had never noticed that passage before, but it seemed to be exactly what I should tell someone who was desperate for help. I remembered John 14:6 as well, where Jesus said, "I am the way …." Bonnie and I prayed again and I dialed the number.

An anxious voice answered, "Hello?"

"Is this John?" I asked. "This is Buck Jacobs. Ted asked me to call."

"Oh, thank God … I need to find God!" the man said. "Can you help me?"

"I can," I said. "Do you have a Bible?"

"I have a Catholic Bible."

"That will work. Go get it and look in St. John, chapter 3, verses 35 and 36, and tell me what it says."

I heard footsteps going away from the phone and then returning.

"Okay, I got it. 'The Father loves the Son and has given all things into His hand. He who believes in the Son has eternal life.' What does that mean?"

"Turn to St. John, chapter 14, and read verse 6," I said.

"I am the way, the truth, and the life," he read, "and no man comes to the Father but by me."

"You see, John, Jesus is the way to find God. Accepting His gift to you through His sacrifice for your sins on the cross is the only way to God."

"But how can I do that?" John cried. "I don't know how!"

"It starts with a simple prayer, John," I said. "Ask Jesus to forgive you for your sins and tell Him that you want to turn away from your past, and then accept His gift and follow Him. If you want that, I can help you. Just follow me and I'll lead you."

John did, and when we finished he began to curse.

"What's wrong, John?" I was shocked.

"I went 16 years to religious schools, and to church for most of my life. This is so simple. Why didn't they tell me?"

"Maybe they did, and you weren't ready to hear, John," I said. "But that's not what's important. Now you know and now you are saved. What really matters is what you do from now on. You can make up for lost time. The past is gone and we can't change it."

John got it, and his whole attitude changed in a second.

"That's right, isn't it? I *am* born again. It's a new start!"

We talked some more, and John grew more and more excited as I shared several verses from Scripture. John joyfully received Christ that night, and we stayed in touch over the next several years. I didn't see him in person until business took me on a prolonged visit to Los Angeles, when Ted hosted a dinner and Bible study at the bakery. John was there with Joe, Roz, and two of Ted's Jewish friends. It was an unforgettable evening and another step in an amazing story.

A few months later when I was at a convention in Palm Springs, I got a call telling me that Ted had suffered a stroke and was not doing well. He was in the UCLA Medical Center. I borrowed a car and drove up to see him. He didn't look good, but he was coherent. We visited and prayed, and he seemed to brighten by the time I left.

I continued to pray on the drive back to Palm Springs and I felt the Lord whisper, "You are going to preach at Ted's funeral." While I drove, I imagined what that might be like. As the miles passed, I grew to know what I would say about my amazing friend. Ted recovered from the stroke and seemed to be doing well, although he was never quite his old feisty self. He was back at the bakery in a few weeks, but I only saw him once more.

Bonnie, the girls, and I returned from a trip to Texas where we saw our son-in-law receive his wings and become an Air Force pilot. As we entered our home, I saw the answering machine light blinking and I had a premonition: *Ted is gone.* Sure enough, Liz had left a message saying that Ted had died the day before, and asked if I would come and speak at his funeral. My mind went back to that drive from LA to Palm Springs. I knew I had to go.

I didn't have much experience preaching at funerals, but I had peace that I was to do this one. I left the next day for LA, and had a good cry with Liz when we met.

We sat on the couch and shared Ted stories with a few relatives who were visiting. Later I asked Liz what she wanted me to do.

"Whatever God tells you to do, Buck, that will be fine. I know Ted will be pleased."

I shared with her the experience I had on that drive long ago, and how I felt that God had told me what I should say if I was asked. She calmly said she knew … God had told her as well. I slept well and was ready the next morning.

The funeral was held in a chapel that was part of an amazing cemetery hidden behind the skyscrapers at Wilshire and Westwood Boulevards in the heart of the Wilshire District, near the UCLA campus. You would never know such a place was there, but many of Hollywood's rich and famous, such as Marilyn Monroe, are buried there. It was truly a stunning atmosphere.

The chapel was full, with about 250 people, and I recognized some well-known stars and personalities. Strangely, I wasn't a bit nervous or intimidated. I delivered the message I had been given, telling those gathered that there were two things I was sure Ted would want them to know. First, he would want them to know how much he had loved his wife, Liz, and what a wonderful partner she had been. I quoted Proverbs 31, which says, "Who can find a virtuous wife? For her worth is far above rubies." I compared Liz's qualities with those God designed, and said I knew Ted would want his life message to be a tribute to his lover and best friend. I told them Ted loved one woman for all of his life, and that he'd often told me so.

Secondly, I told them Ted would want them to know he was with his Lord, and would not want them to mourn. Instead, he would want them to look forward to seeing him again. I told them how Ted had helped me find my way to God in Jesus, and how they could do so as well. I closed by inviting them to know Christ and led them in a prayer of repentance and acceptance of the free gift of salvation in Jesus.

It was funny, in a way, but as I closed I realized I didn't know what to do next. There was no clergy present, and the funeral director was standing at the back of the church like he knew that I knew what to do. So I stepped down from the lectern, walked to the back of the church, and out the door. One of the assistants directed me to the gravesite, assuming we would have a gravesite prayer. He motioned me towards an open grave across the field, about 100 yards away through the trees. I started to walk across as they wheeled Ted's casket to a waiting hearse. I turned to look back as I walked and was surprised to see that the people were slowly following me. It was really a solemn and beautiful sight.

When I arrived at the graveside, one of Ted's actor friends whom I knew was a Christian Jew, came up to me and introduced his estranged wife.

"Marilyn has just been diagnosed with incurable throat cancer," he said. "Would you pray for her to be healed?"

"I will," I replied. "But first, Marilyn, did you hear what I said in the service about accepting Jesus as Lord and Savior?"

She smiled and said she did.

"Wouldn't you like to know you are safe with Him, before I ask Him to heal your body?"

"Yes," she said immediately. "I would. I want that."

Standing there next to my dear friend's grave with scores of strangers standing as … what? Witnesses? I don't know, but I do know that Marilyn gave her heart to Jesus right there. She actually glowed and wept tears of joy as she asked Jesus to forgive her and cleanse her heart. When she finished, I laid my hands on her and asked Jesus to also be her healer.

I led the mourners in a short prayer of committal as Ted was lowered into the ground … actually not him, but his used "earth suit." We mingled a while longer and left.

According to her doctors, Marilyn had been given six months to live. But the last I heard of her was several years later and she was cancer free. What a fitting sendoff for Ted. I was so amazed at God's Grace. I have visited Ted's grave a few times over the years, and can still see it all in my mind's eye … even now. To think it all started with me watching two guys play backgammon by the pool one Saturday morning. God used Ted to reach me, and then me to reach back to Ted, and then through Ted to…. only He knows. That's pretty radical, don't you think?

Chapter 9

Surprise! The Business Is Sold – A New Life in Florida

Life can change in the blink of an eye.

One morning in 1983, Bob stepped into my office and told me he had decided to sell the business. I was shocked, and he was not kidding. He said he believed God was redirecting his life and that he would move to Texas to work with an evangelist. Within a month he sold the business to one of our team members, and then Bob was gone.

Although at first I didn't agree with his decision, I later realized it might be a good thing. Bob had become discouraged with the business for reasons I won't go into, and recently he'd not made decisions that should have been made in a more timely fashion. The buyer promised to make some necessary changes and told me that unless I would agree to stay, he wouldn't go through with the deal. As things turned out, I wasn't sure if he meant that or if it was merely a ploy on his part. At this point it doesn't really matter, and I will probably never know. I do know that the sale and transfer of ownership was the beginning of one of the hardest years of my life.

To start, the new owner stripped most of the Christian activities from the business. His excuse was that we weren't living up to the professional standards of a Christian company in a perfect way, and until we could (as if anyone ever had or could), we shouldn't be so assertive about it. Next, the Bible studies were stopped and the Scripture verses were removed from the labels and barrels. Then the words "Jesus is Lord" were taken off the side of the building. While these things don't define a Christian business, they were all key components that had been the result of prayer, and were a significant element of the company's culture. The mood changed quickly—very quickly—and it became progressively clearer that I really didn't fit anymore.

A decision point came for me when I was called in to the new owner's office and told that I needed to reduce the sales department budget by one third. He said I needed to do so by cutting out two people. The catch was that I could only cut people who had less seniority with the business than I did. It was a silly condition that accomplished only one thing: it protected one of the new owner's friends who had worked in the business for a few years longer than I had. That man was not a strong Christian, nor was he a significant producer, and it would mean I had to let go two men who were both. It wasn't fair and I recognized the manipulation behind his actions. I was given a few days to let him know whom I would let go.

I never imagined leaving the Mack Company, and thought I would be there until I retired. But as Bonnie and I prayed, we felt the Lord's leading that I should resign rather than do what I had been asked to do. There were several reasons. First, the men who would be let go had left good jobs to join the company and they would be adversely affected financially if they were terminated. They were good brothers in the Lord who were high-producing teammates. I didn't feel I could be a part of the decision to let them go just to protect the job of the owner's friend who didn't measure up. Second, the atmosphere and culture of the business had changed substantially. What seemed like unimportant changes—even justified changes at the time they were introduced—had a stifling effect on the attitudes and practices within the team. People were afraid and became political and insecure. The attitude of the new leader was a departure from our foundation. His changes pumped up the profit-and-loss statements and removed most of Jesus' influence from the business. I really didn't want to stay.

I went to the meeting and shocked the owner by resigning. I only asked for time to make a final tour of our customers to thank them for their business. It would take about a month. I pointed out that my compensation would almost equal the reduction he had asked for. I sensed that while he was very surprised at my decision to leave my six-figure position and the perks that had accrued over time, he was also relieved. The two of us had been close (I thought) before he became the owner, and I believed he was as committed to the concept of a Christian business as I. But I had been wrong. He was a politician at heart, who played the game very well. He was out for what was best for him and not really aligned with Bob's philosophy. He agreed to my proposal, and I made plans for a "thanks and goodbye" tour. I had no idea what I would do next, but as soon as I made the decision, I felt the burden was lifted.

During my final month, a brother from our church approached me for some advice. He ran the sales component of a company that was growing very quickly, and needed help in organizing the activities and management of a sales team. He was a very good salesman but had no sales management background. When he found out I would be leaving the Mack Company, he asked me to join him as a consultant / sales manager for a season. I accepted, stayed with him for a year, and the business prospered.

That year, I had to decide how I might—or might not—capitalize on the fact that I didn't have a noncompete agreement with the Mack Company. It was highly unusual that I wasn't bound by such a contract, but we had never used them and I suppose the new owner never thought to ask for one—which I would have gladly signed. Not having such an agreement meant I could have cut a deal with any of our competitors for whatever I could get. I had knowledge that would potentially be worth millions of dollars to them. I knew every person in every key account in the market, both in R&D and in the production plants. And I knew the formulary and suppliers of our proprietary products. I didn't know the exact proportions, but that wasn't important because just knowing "what and who" supplied the ingredients would have been extremely helpful to the competition. At the time, Mack held about 40% of the worldwide share of this market niche.

In the end, it really wasn't a hard decision. It was bad enough watching the Christ-centered culture that we had built in the Mack Company be gradually drained away, but I couldn't imagine working for a company that took the business from the Mack Company. Nor could I face the customers I had witnessed to for so many years and worked so closely with, as the new representative of a non-Christian supplier. I left a lot of money on the table, yet I have never questioned the decision. By violating a *moral* noncompete, I would have violated my own standard of integrity as well as that of the Lord Jesus … if I had done such a thing just for the money.

There was something else; I never liked the chemical business, anyway. It was learning to understand business from a Christian perspective that was what I treasured. It wasn't the money. I had never asked Bob for a raise or done anything other than say "Thank you" when he changed my compensation over the years. I trusted God to provide, and believed He was doing so through Bob. Our income had grown a bunch, and while we had some savings, our standard of living hardly changed. No, it wasn't about money; it was all about serving the Lord. I could do that in my new job, with my friend, in his sales organization. I couldn't do that with any of the competitors … not at all!

***

Over the last three years at the Mack Company I had gotten involved with a group of Christian professional golfers from the PGA Tour. Through those relationships, Bonnie and I got to know a couple from Michigan we'd met at a Christian Pro-Am Tournament. We vacationed together a couple of times and really hit it off. We dreamed of someday starting a Christian golf course—a place staffed and run by Christians, and with an atmosphere of loving service that would cause people to ask about it. We would then have "earned" the ability to tell them about Jesus. In our dreams, we described all the ways that the customers would be touched and the community blessed.

It was a fun, exciting dream. We thought we might develop a golf community near the course, which would attract people who weren't Christians as well as those who were. We kept in touch with some members of the Tour Bible Study and talked to them about the concept. We found that some of them had been thinking about the same thing.

Towards the end of that year, I got a call from my friend in Michigan. He excitedly explained that while vacationing in Florida he had met an acquaintance from Michigan, a PGA professional named Tom. Over dinner they discussed the dream of a Christian golf community. Tom told Joe that he had just bought an 18-hole golf course in a place called Apollo Beach, south of Tampa, Florida. He invited Joe to consider applying the idea of Christian ministry through golf at his course. Joe told him about me, and they invited me to visit the course and talk, which I did.

It was an out-of-the-way location in a very small community, but the course was first rate and the new friendship with Tom came easily. It was soon obvious that he was a serious Christian who wanted to see golf used to help win the world for Christ and would make a great partner in our effort. We formed a nonprofit corporation called The Golf and Sea Fellowship.

I found a home near the course and made a purchase offer that was accepted. Bonnie had never seen the home, yet she gave me the go-ahead based on my description. Talk about faith! What a great partner she was, and has been throughout our journey together. We put our Illinois home on the market and sold it within a couple of weeks. Then, in less time than you could believe, we were packed in a U-Haul truck and on our way to a new life. It would be a life that I thought I knew, but really didn't have a clue about—the life of faith. A life where there is no one and nothing else to trust but God, in Jesus.

From the time I gave my heart to Jesus and told Him I would do whatever He wanted me to do with the rest of my life, I had been learning to trust the Lord more and more, one step at a time. Starting with tithing when it looked like it would only hasten bankruptcy, to the fire at the plant, the financial miracle of the survival and eventual prosperity of the business, Bonnie and I had almost countless opportunities to see God work and supply our needs. He had built our trust in His faithfulness to meet us, care for our needs, and answer tons of prayers for ourselves and others. We had seen many family members and others saved and healed of serious illness, and had been given financial abundance, which in turn taught us the blessing of giving.

Except for the first year at the Mack Company, I had a salary plus bonus and commissions. As the business grew and our situation became more and more stable, our need to trust God for our finances lessened. We never thought of it that way and we regarded our prosperity as God's blessing. But both Bonnie and I recognized we had lost something precious. The decision to move to Florida was, in a large part, to regain the need to trust God. Moving to a new community to do something I had never done, with a limited ability to financially provide, seemed to be God's direction for us. I never felt the golf ministry was my highest or final call, but I saw that it would be a good thing ... a step towards where God was leading us.

We made some money when the chemical business sold. So when it came time to move to Florida, the equity from the house that God gave us, coupled with our savings, was enough to pay cash for our house. We had become debt free and still had enough left to live on for a year or two if we were careful. I assumed that either the golf ministry would grow and be able to pay a salary, or I would find a job to support the family. Things had been going so easily in the Lord that I *assumed* they would continue. Bonnie and I were certain God had called us to this move, but I was in for "graduate school in living by faith" and didn't know it.

The first "curve ball" happened within two weeks of our arrival. Our partner, Joe, announced he was leaving for a three-month RV trip across the country. He had never mentioned that as a possibility before we moved down there. Tom was busy rebuilding the watering system on the golf course, so now it was up to me to get the ministry of The Golf and Sea Fellowship off the ground. Of course I had no experience or training on how to do that.

When you reflect on this story, I'm sure you'll see God's pattern in my life of putting me in positions where, if they worked out, I could never take credit but would be sure to see His hand of provision. But the lessons were only beginning. I have always been inadequate for every task He has given me and never felt I could do it alone. In every case, though, something deep within urged me to step out of my comfort zone and seize what seemed to be in front of me day by day. That's what I did in this situation, and God got the golf ministry launched and prospering.

We found that golf was a great way to draw a disparate group of people together. Many of them had a relationship of some sort with God, or at least had an openness to explore a relationship with Him. We had community golf on Saturday afternoons where we gave free golf to anyone who came, and asked only that they bring a dish for a potluck dinner afterwards. At dinner, we said grace and offered a short devotion, relating some aspect of the game of golf with some focus on the Gospel. We found that many of the people who believed in God, for a variety of reasons didn't go to church. Several of them told us that if there were a church "like our golf fellowship," they would come. So a church was planted and it grew to nearly 100 members in the course of three years. We named it Apollo Beach Community Church.

We held couples golf retreats and started the "Church Challenge Cup" event, where local churches could enter teams with two believers and two nonbelievers (or wavering members), and compete for a traveling Cup. The winning church would keep the Cup, have their name engraved on it, and bring it back to defend it at the next event. We soon reached full capacity for this event and saw some come to Christ or recommit their lives to Jesus almost every time. We even saw a miraculous healing.

While all this was going on, I was deeply engaged in the "school of faith." The golf ministry didn't require a lot of time since it was event-driven work with time between events. So I began to look for work, at first part-time, and then as the ministry solidified and our funds dwindled, something more permanent. I thought it would be easy to find work, but it didn't turn out that way. I was either too old, too qualified, or too whatever. After sending out countless résumés over two years and following every lead, I had exactly zero offers. I can still remember the day I cashed the last of our money market funds. I thought, *Well, God, I'll really have to trust You now.* I had no clue how much trust would be required, since I was still confident I would find a job.

I was about to find out and learn more about my true Source.

Chapter 10
Miracles of Provision and Direction in Florida

Two years after we moved to Florida I hadn't found any work, apart from a couple of short consulting jobs. Our bank account began to bump up against zero. I wasn't really worried because I had seen God provide at the last minute before. But I still didn't know what to do. One day I was walking on our treadmill on the pool deck in the heat of the summer, sweating like mad and practicing the ancient art of grumbling, handed down from our spiritual ancestors.

"God, what's the deal?" I asked. "I came here to serve You and now I'm broke and have no idea where to go next. What do you want me to do?"

I haven't heard God speak clearly in my heart very often, but as soon as I asked the question, I heard God say to me, *Buck, what do you need today?*

It took me aback. I wasn't really expecting Him to answer me … not with a question like that. But it caused me to reflect for a moment. *Our bills are paid, we have plenty of food, and Bonnie and the girls are healthy.*

"Nothing, Lord," I said. "I have everything I need today."

Then, what are you worried about? I heard.

I thought of the King James version of the Bible, in Matthew 6:34, which says, "Sufficient unto the day is the evil thereof." I realized I did have much to be grateful for. I remembered that worrying is the same as borrowing the future's troubles, so I laughed at myself and tried to take the lesson to heart. It didn't put a dollar in my account, but the lesson was far more valuable.

Shortly after that, an old friend from Illinois came to spend a week with us. While she was at our home, I got a call from a man who had been one of our can lube customers. He asked me to come to Denver to interview for a job. I had no desire to work for his company, let alone move to Denver, but I also knew who had recommended me for the job. So out of respect and because I knew and liked Dick, I told the man I would come to Denver for an interview.

It happened that on the same day our friend was flying back to Illinois, I was leaving for Denver, so we drove to the airport together. Before we left, Bonnie, our friend, and I stood in a circle praying and thanking God for His blessing of friendship and for our time together.

I was led to pray, "Lord, You know that I really don't want to go to Denver, so please use me to share Your good news on the trip to make it worthwhile."

As we finished, our friend said she really felt that God would answer my request in a special way. I left with a feeling of excitement and high expectations.

In my time of travel with the Mack Company, God had used me to witness many times with people I sat next to on planes, met in plants or hotel lobbies, or who were hitchhikers, cab drivers, and so on. The world around us is hurting. If we're alert, God will use us in lives which—only in the eternal sense—are incidental to our being there. So I was very alert on the plane, in the cab on the way to the hotel, and with the staff checking in. But I got no responses to my probing questions. There was nothing the next morning at breakfast either, so I went off to the interview.

The company was a large business known to be employee friendly. They wanted to extend and leverage technology that they had developed and incorporated, into their own production process. They had formed a new division, and appointed as their president, the man who'd called me. He was putting a staff together and I had been recommended for the position of vice president of sales.

I would have been a perfect choice since I knew every one of his potential customers very well from my experience with the Mack Company. And the company would have been an excellent, although secular, employer. The only problems I had were the Denver location and the fact that I wanted nothing more to do with the chemical business.

The president pitched the opportunity to me very well and then as a good recruiter does, asked the committing question.

"Where do you see yourself in this picture, Buck?"

"I'm really sorry, Dick, but I just don't see myself there at all," I replied.

"Why not?" he asked.

"Well, I just moved my family to Florida two years ago and I don't want to ask them to move again. And besides, I hate the chemical business."

"What do you mean, you hate the chemical business? You were so successful in it, and you even sold us. Why do you say that?"

"I didn't pick the chemical business for myself … God picked it for me. And the reason I stayed until after it was sold wasn't because I had any love for the business, it was because of the challenge and opportunity to work in a Christian business that was trying to operate using biblical principles. That part I loved."

"That's interesting," Dick replied. "Maybe we can talk more over lunch."

He went on to discuss other things for a few minutes, and then we drove to a restaurant.

At lunch I felt prompted to offer him an alternative. "Dick, you don't really need to hire me or anyone else for this job at this point. You don't know what products you will develop or what the overall market is looking for. Why don't you consider hiring me as a consultant? I can work for you from my home part-time and I can revisit all of my contacts. That way I can survey them to understand where their needs are greatest, and help you focus your product development towards their collective sweet spots."

I could tell he was paying close attention. I continued. "Later, when things are more defined, I can help you find the right person for your job."

"Would you be interested in that kind of relationship?" Dick asked.

I said I would be excited to help him, and that it might be the best of both worlds for each of us. Dick was thoughtful for several moments.

"Tell me more about the 'Christian business' thing you mentioned. What does that look like?"

"Let me ask you a question, Dick. Do you consider yourself to be a born-again Christian?" I asked.

"I'm not sure."

"Then you're not," I replied. "Everyone who is born again knows it."

"How did it happen for you?" Dick asked.

I told him how I met the Lord, Bob's call, and several of our experiences over the years of seeing God's provision and guidance in the business. Dick listened attentively, not asking many questions but obviously very much into our conversation. I didn't push him about his faith any further, and then finished my explanation.

"So you see, Dick, an exciting adventure with God started with that simple prayer in my living room, and I don't want to let it go."

He suggested we leave and go visit some of the other employees I had known. We spent the rest of the afternoon and throughout dinner in other discussions, and there was no further opportunity to talk about Jesus. But my antennae were up, and I sensed that God was answering my prayer to be used on this trip.

On the way back to my hotel, Dick was quiet for a while.

"Would you mind if I told you something personal?" he said.

"Of course not."

"Yesterday, I realized I had bitten off more than I could chew in this new position," he said. "I'm a scientist, not an executive, and I realized I was going to fail. After dinner I started to try to tell my wife what I had discerned, but I couldn't get it out. I began to sob uncontrollably. I couldn't talk. I just went into our bedroom and lay down on the bed and began to cry out, 'God help me, God help me' until I fell asleep."

I listened while this man poured his heart out.

"Then I got up this morning and came to work to meet with you, and all you wanted to tell me is about how you met God, how He has helped you, and how Jesus changed your life. I want you to know that you didn't come here to get a job. God sent you here for me."

"Well, Dick," I said, "he's only one simple prayer away from you."

I didn't feel I should go further at that point, but just to let God continue to deal with Dick. I know some would say I should have asked him to pray with me right then, and I can't really argue with that. I've done so, many times, but I sensed this was not the time.

We shook hands and agreed to talk in a few days.

Dick called me a couple of days later, and when I asked how he was doing, he replied, "Great! Since you were here, everything's changed."

"What's changed?" I asked.

"Everything."

"Can I ask you a personal question, Dick?"

"Sure."

"Do you consider yourself a born-again Christian?"

"I sure do," was his reply.

Dick was right. God didn't send me to Denver for a job. He had a much bigger purpose in mind. Dick and his wife (who already knew the Lord) joined a church. The next time I visited, they were singing in the choir together. So a wonderful friendship began—a friendship that we will take up in Heaven. And, by the way, Dick loved the idea of my working with them on a consulting basis. We signed a simple agreement to do so.

Over the next two years, the income from that agreement became the primary source of sustenance that God used to meet our family's needs. When the checkbook would be about to run out, an assignment came through from Dick. It was helpful to him as well, and he didn't fail in his position either.

In this same period of time, I learned that the Fellowship of Companies for Christ International (FCCI) was beginning a small group extension to their seminar ministry. One of the test areas they had selected was Tampa. I went to their next monthly meeting and introduced myself to the leaders as a former founding member of FCCI. They were very new to the concept and eagerly invited me to share some of my experiences from my Mack Company days. We had been founding members of FCCI since we first heard of them, and had hosted a small group of 15 or so local business owners at twice-per-month meetings at our plant in Illinois. I had way more background with the organization than they did, so I got "volunteered" into helping with local leadership … which I was thrilled to do.

At the next monthly meeting I was seated next to a man named Martin Newby. That arrangement would prove to be a life-changing event, although as usual I had no clue of this at the time. At the end of the meeting, Martin said the FCCI concept was a great idea and asked if we could do the same thing in Sarasota. I said yes. He asked what they should do to get started, and I told him FCCI had an introductory video and that I would get him a copy. I told him he could invite all the Christian business owners he knew to come to a luncheon or breakfast and show it to them. Those who wanted to, could join and hold meetings in Sarasota.

"I'm no good in front of a group," said Martin. "Would you come and explain FCCI for us?"

I agreed to do so. Two weeks later I arrived at the Ramada Inn by the Sarasota Airport and went into a conference room filled with about 40 Christian business owners. We showed the video. Afterwards, one group decided to meet in Sarasota and another one planned to meet in nearby Bradenton. Then, Martin told them that I would lead the groups! He has always been very good at delegating.

The Tampa group asked me to provide leadership for smaller groups there, as well as for a large monthly group luncheon. The latter was soon discontinued in favor of multiple small groups that met in areas across the Tampa / St. Petersburg bay area. One of the members in the Tampa group had a brother-in-law in DeLand, a small city north of Orlando. When he told him how he had enjoyed our group in Tampa, the brother-in-law asked if they could start one there. He said he didn't know how it worked, but he would "ask the guy who leads us." And that's how I found myself in DeLand a week later, showing the video to a dozen friends of Frank, the brother-in-law.

And so it went. Spontaneously and without any effort or intention, within three months, six groups had formed. They were spread across Central Florida, down the west coast, and across to Miami, and they met each week. I was the de facto leader of all of them. Apparently, I fit the classic definition of an expert—someone who was from over 50 miles away and who carried a briefcase.

I had the advantage of possessing videotapes from previous FCCI conferences, as well as some Larry Burkett (of business book fame) audiotapes. These were the resources that got me through those early days. I would often pray while driving to one of the meetings, for guidance on what to teach or share that day. Jesus always provided, often with something related to a local situation that I didn't know about. Members occasionally asked, "How did you know I needed to hear that?" I simply said, "I didn't, but Jesus did."

One day I went to the mailbox and found a box of business cards from FCCI. "Area Coordinator" was printed below my name. I called the FCCI office in Atlanta and asked the general manager what that meant. He said, "We were hoping you would tell us." He said they had been hearing good things about what was happening and just wanted me to keep it up, and be available to answer questions or give literature to folks who inquired in Florida. I was glad to do so.

Things kept hopping along and in a few months we had nine groups. Then I got another call from FCCI saying they had located two other men who were doing what I was, and wondered if I would be willing to come to Atlanta to meet with them. Some members of the FCCI Board also would be there. They wanted to formalize a way of working together and develop a model that would be used by FCCI as it expanded into other states. I agreed, and a couple of weeks later I drove to Atlanta. I met with a man from Denver and another from Cleveland, along with the FCCI folks. Together, we hammered out an organizational model that looked a bit like a franchise. The model required a Board of Directors to support and raise funds for the work locally, and then report to the national headquarters. The plan was a bit rough, but it was a start.

When I returned from Atlanta I called Martin and outlined what we had discussed. I asked if he would lead the task of putting together our Florida Board to support me as the FCCI Area Coordinator for the state. He agreed, and since then, Martin has been a key friend and supporter of my work. Without Martin and my wife, I know that the eventual launch of The C12 Group would never have happened.

About that time, a "tipping point" came into my life in the form of a personal challenge from God. One day while I was preparing to lead a planning seminar for a member company, I had one of the "still, small voice" experiences that I have learned to recognize as Jesus speaking to me in a very personal way. I heard: *Buck, if you want to be effective in the lives of others, I want the first hour of your day.*

I immediately knew what He was talking about. For several years I had struggled to have a consistent and meaningful daily quiet time with the Lord … a time of Bible study, prayer, reflection, and listening for that still, small voice. I had studied the lives of many great Christians, and for years had recognized that every one of them spoke of the need for, and value of, a quiet hour with God in the morning. People like Mother Teresa, George Müller, Hudson Taylor, and others that I greatly admired and wanted to emulate, all said the same thing: They couldn't have done what they had without the strength and guidance they received during their first-hour discipline. I had tried but failed to apply the principle many times. I am more of a night person than a morning person, and the temptation to sleep in always tripped me up.

Somehow I knew this was different, that it was a pivot point for me. I had to make a clear choice to obey or disobey, and I sensed my future would be determined by my choice. I did want to be effective—no doubt about that. So I asked God to show me how to do it, and told Him I would try again. Again I heard the still, small voice: *Make it nonnegotiable.* I got it. No more daily decision making as to whether to get up and spend time with Him or not. The first hour belongs to Him and I need to spend it with Him. I committed in my heart to start the next morning, before realizing that in a few days I would be staying in a condo on Longboat Key with Bonnie and the girls. I didn't know our accommodations would be a single, one-bedroom unit with a pull-out bed, and that the only place I could go to have that first hour without waking them would be the bathroom.

When we arrived at the condo and I saw the arrangements, I realized that my first hour would be a bit uncomfortable. But that wasn't the point; the point was to do it. The first hour was His, period. I had to be at breakfast with our hosts at 7:30 AM, and that meant I had to be in the shower by seven. So the first hour with the Lord would be from 6:00 to 7:00 AM … early for me, but still doable.

As I set the alarm for 6:00 AM before turning off the light, I thought to pray: "Lord, please wake me before the alarm so I don't have to bother the girls." I turned off the light and the next thing I remember was opening my eyes and looking at the digital clock. It read 5:59 AM. I knew God had given me a personal pat on the back, a sign that I could clearly recognize as from Him. It was His encouragement to "press on" in a discipline that would become a great blessing.

That was over 9,500 days ago—almost 30 years. I know this because on that day I began to journal my thoughts; I wrote a list of things I was grateful for. I started in my journal as: "Day #1: Thank you, Father, for …." The next morning I wrote: "Day #2: Thank you, Father, for …," and so on. I've kept that practice as part of my daily routine ever since. I stop for a minute to think about what I have to be thankful for in the last 24 hours, and then I write them down. It's amazing. We take so much for granted, yet God blesses us every day. Through the years I have only missed four or five days because of travel on long, overnight flights. But the key has been that my first hour belongs to God, and He wants me to spend it with Him. No other decision—after the decision to accept Jesus—has so dramatically changed my life.

My quiet-time discipline has been the foundation for all that God has done through me in the years since. And He continues to lead me in His will through areas where I know I am not prepared and am unable to go without Him. He has used it to build what has become my life's work, The C12 Group. Nothing that I have taught or shared with others—this quiet time with the Lord in the morning—has blessed or changed their lives more … as many have told me through the years. The simple key was to make the first hour nonnegotiable. I have slipped a few times and allowed other things to creep into my day before settling in to be with my Father. But He has always gently shown me how unimportant the other things are in comparison. Then I tell Him I'm sorry for slipping, and get back to keeping first things first. There is no practice, no study, and no tool that I can recommend more highly than to live a 24-hour day and give the first hour back to Him.

Over the next five years the FCCI work flourished, both in Florida and across the U.S. That's the good news. The better news is that while the work flourished, the financial support did not.

The Florida FCCI Board set a budget each year that included a modest salary for me. But in six years we never met the budget. Of course when we fell short, it was only my salary that didn't get paid since we always paid our obligations, including a tithe of all income, first. We never missed or were late paying a bill, or shorted a tithe, but most often it was the salary account that took a hit. Why was that better news? Because God used those months and years to show my family how He could sovereignly meet our needs in many other ways. Our girls, Leah and Sarah, were seven and nine years old when we moved. We always included them as much as possible in praying for our needs, and then shared with them God's answers. There were countless examples of this. Following are a handful that come to mind.

One:

Our roof began to leak during the afternoon showers that are part of Florida summers, and we had no money to repair it. Bonnie, being the resourceful trooper that she is, would put a bucket under the spot that leaked. When more leaks appeared, she added more buckets, until one day we had more leaks than buckets. I mentioned our need at one of our FCCI meetings, and the next day a brother from another city called and said, "I hear you need a new roof." I told him we did, and he said, "God told me to provide one for you. Get a couple of quotes, pick the best one, and let me know how much it costs. I'll send you a check."

Two:

I was visiting one of our group leaders at his home and he asked me if my girls would be offended if they were given hand-me-down clothes. I told him "Not at all," and he led me into the other room, where he and his wife had collected two large garbage bags full of clothes. Their daughters were a couple of years older than ours and had stopped wearing the clothes. They planned to give them to Goodwill. I carried them home, and you would have thought that Christmas came early to our house as the girls pulled item after item from the bags. Some were designer labels that we would never have been able to buy, while others had the price tags still attached. The girls were thrilled, as they learned about Jehovah-jireh … the God who provides.

Three:

I was an avid racquetball player in those days, and ran to keep in shape. A couple of Christian brothers and I used to "beat each other's brains out" three times a week on the courts, and then I ran on the off days. My running shoes were a wreck, but I had no money to replace them. I made do, until we went to a church picnic where I shared with an attorney friend about my dilemma.

"I'm a runner too," he said, "and I have sensitive feet. What size do you wear?"

I told him size 10, and he said to stop by his house on the way home.

"I've got some that I've tried," he said, "and they hurt my feet. Maybe you can use them."

We stopped at his house, and he took me into the garage where he handed me a garbage bag half-full of running shoes. Almost all new, all size 10. "Take them," he said. "I'll never use them."

Twelve or more pairs … is that abundance or what? I picked out two or three pairs and shared the rest with others in need. I had them for years.

Four:

Others provided me with travel to conventions or offered beautiful beach homes for our vacations. Money came in to purchase repairs on cars that never broke down except in our driveway or near a service station in town. We purchased used cars that I drove for thousands and thousands of miles around Florida, and they never once broke down on the road. Bonnie had the same protection as she carried the girls to school events in cars that had very high mileage.

Five:

Our air conditioner quit in the middle of a Florida summer, and we had no money for a replacement. When Bonnie told the serviceman about our mission and our circumstances, he told her to wait a minute. He left and came back with a replacement motor that he had taken from another unit, and sold it to us for $10. It ran for 13 years, and was still running when we sold the house.

Six:

One of our biggest challenges was paying for our girls' college education. As you can imagine, we had no money, and as they progressed through their high school years it became a matter of almost daily prayer at our morning family devotions. It's a much longer story, but Sarah received a full voice scholarship to Brenau University in Gainesville, Georgia—a Christian school none of us had ever heard of. Her sister, Leah, followed her there two years later on a leadership scholarship. Both girls had an amazing college experience at Brenau. Both met their husbands there and both became schoolteachers. They taught for two years together after graduating. Neither they, nor we, had one dollar of debt upon graduation.

Beyond God's amazing provision, I was also learning to trust Him in ways I couldn't have imagined. Once, I drove five hours across Florida to conduct a Fellowship of Companies for Christ International (FCCI) lunch introduction that was scheduled by a man in Titusville. I arrived a bit early and sat in the meeting room at the restaurant, waiting for him and his guests. No one showed up. Noon came and went, and when I called his number, no one answered. I waited another hour, ate lunch, and left. Driving home, I was discouraged and frustrated. In my spirit I grumbled, *What's the deal, Lord? I drove all these hours for nothing. The guy is a jerk. What a waste of time!*

Again in my spirit, I heard a question: *Buck, were you prepared to do what I asked you to do? Were you diligent to be ready to share?*

I reviewed my prep work and readiness. *Yes, Lord, I was ready. I could have done what You asked as well as I could.*

Then, that is all you are responsible for. I will take the responsibility for the numbers.

I got it. God is my Source, not man. My responsibility is to pray up, suit up, and show up. The rest is up to Him. That lesson has stayed with me and has seen me through many other situations where others have failed to produce as they promised—even in situations such as guests not coming to a C12 meeting when they said they would. It's a great lesson: All God asks of us is our obedience, while He takes responsibility for the results. The deal is to try to learn God's will and do it as well as we can day by day.

Each day is its own test. If, and when, we rest our heads on the pillow at the end of each day, we can be at peace knowing we have done the best we could in His will. Then we rest assured that He will always provide all we need in order to do everything He truly asks of us.

Chapter 11
C12 Starts – A Dream Opens

After five years of FCCI work, I discerned that the model for the groups we were using was seriously flawed and we needed to make some changes. I wasn't upset with anyone else since I was the one primarily responsible for the model. But the groups just kept cycling in new members to replace others that so easily dropped off, and we had no way to know whether our work was being effective in their businesses. The relatively low "skin in the game" and accountability of our voluntary gifts-based payment model didn't seem to serve others as well as I had hoped. By that time, I was in charge of training leaders for FCCI. I knew that 90% of our area leaders were starving for lack of support and eventually would leave if nothing changed.

I was aware of a secular CEO roundtable model that helped business CEOs and owners, and required a monthly fee for membership. It seemed to me that if we could adapt such a fee-for-service model and make it biblical and Christ-centered while providing the same level of value, Christians would participate in such a group. In addition, I had always felt that FCCI should provide a more business-focused format that would be truly practical and helpful in the business dimension of their work. Such a model would, at the same time, encourage members to recognize the true eternal purpose of their business. The model would equip company owners and CEOs to "build great businesses for a greater purpose"—a phrase that later became our C12 tag line. It would also encourage them to look at business as a vehicle for ministry in the same way I had learned at the Mack Company.

I analyzed the effectiveness of my work with FCCI, and realized that businesses which were most able to focus on ministry were the larger ones that provided a stable "platform" from which to reach others. They had also been the most faithful and were able to support the group financially. Those types of businesses had grown to the point where the owners were able to delegate and "leave the company" for a day, based on having at least a rudimentary management team in their place. They were focused on growing their businesses rather than just earning a paycheck and having a place to go to work. Those were the businesses I wanted to focus on working with in the new model.

I first proposed my draft model to FCCI, thinking it would meet the needs that I knew were there. But I was surprised and disappointed when they essentially turned down my offer. I was faced with the decision of whether to stay and implement a model that I didn't believe was particularly effective, or leave to start an independent organization that would work at a higher and deeper level. Even though my support as FCCI's area coordinator was sporadic, it was a fairly secure lifestyle, so the decision was by no means easy. Sarah was about to start her freshman year in college, and Leah was two years behind her. After much prayer and counsel we decided to leave FCCI and start The C12 Group as a fee-for-service, for-profit business.

Humble Beginnings

God's direction was clear, so I resigned from FCCI in 1992, at the age 54. My new office would be in my home. For my desk, Bonnie found a used door and two double-drawer file cabinets at a garage sale and placed the door on top of them. We bought a fax machine and had a business phone installed on one side of our family / TV room. And that's where we set up shop.

The Lord had provided two beta test groups—both started in October 1992. He blessed us with a third, launched in January of 1993, but we still had no C12 literature and no source of study materials. When I had developed the design for FCCI, I had assumed they would provide content, so when I left I thought I would just find another source. I'd used materials from my book, *A Light Shines Bright in Babylon: A Handbook for Christian Business Owners*, for the first month. But by the second month, I knew I was in trouble and had to find another source. One day, I was in a car dealer's service waiting room for what I expected would be a couple of hours, so I began to pray. I asked the Lord for a source for study materials, and I thought

I heard Him say, *You write them.* I couldn't believe that was Him, so I was quiet for a while. Then it came back. *You write them.*

"But Lord," I prayed, "I am not a writer, and I have never written anything but the book You gave me. I'm not qualified. Many of the members will be much smarter than I am, and have much more experience with bigger companies. I can't do it."

Just then, I got the hint of an idea. I took a tablet and pen from my briefcase and began to rough out some thoughts. By the time I left, I had a good bit of a teaching segment and even an idea for a companion piece. I went home and worked into the night, and again the next day. I took the draft to my volunteer secretary, who typed them and duplicated them for me. When I took them to the next scheduled group meeting, I fully expected to be laughed out of the room.

But the meeting went well and afterwards two or three members stopped me to say that the materials were "good this month." The same thing happened with the next two groups. I was amazed and humbled. I knew God had encouraged me to write the materials, but the question was, *Would He ever do so again?*

The next month I prayed again and asked Him what He wanted to say to the groups. Again, the gentle hint of an idea came to me. I sat right down and began to work on it, and God provided. At the next meeting, all the members were there and several remarked favorably that the material was helpful. I also began to see confirmation of its effect when I met with the members personally each month (the one-on-one element of the monthly C12 process) and saw that they were working to apply the concepts. They asked questions that showed me they had been thinking deeply about the materials. Thus began the pattern that went on for over nine years. I would write materials, use them that month, and immediately begin to pray for the next month's studies.

Sometimes, God gave me ideas in very creative ways. Bonnie and I would go on Friday night dates to a bookstore and I would walk up and down the Business Books or Christian Books sections, praying, "God, what do You want to say to the groups this month?" A hint of an idea would direct my eye to the title of a book—sometimes two or more. I had become a strategic reader, and I always looked for something that would spark a new learning experience for the groups. I focused on both business development and spiritual dimensions—whether for the personal needs of the leader or for their business.

Writing the curriculum was a wonderful time of personal spiritual development for me. I knew I wasn't qualified to do what I was doing, and if God didn't supply, I was toast. But He did supply, and the reaction of the members confirmed it was from Him. His supply of the study materials through me—a guy with only a high school degree—to groups that included men with MBAs from schools like Wharton and Harvard, was one of the clearest evidences that C12 was God's. Again, He had put me in a place where I knew that I was unqualified and could never take credit, and then did through me what I knew I couldn't do apart from Jesus.

It is so wonderful to have that sense of intimacy and dependency on our Father! He used this facet of our relationship to grow me in so many ways. I knew I couldn't give to others what I didn't have myself, and I needed to stay close to Jesus if I wanted to urge them to do so. My quiet times also deepened and lengthened, and I pleaded with Him to hold my hand and keep me close. We had seen God as the supplier of our financial and sustenance needs, but now I was learning to go deeper and more fully know Him as the Source of all.

I had three criteria that I felt were God-given as I sought to measure the effectiveness of the C12 model. First, do the members stay in the groups? I knew from my own experience that no CEO or business owner would continue to spend one day every month away from their business—and pay to do it—unless they were receiving real value. The members would vote with their feet. But at the end of the first year, 80% of the members who started were still in their groups and going strong. Only one member in the first two years left saying he didn't receive value from his C12 experience, and he returned after a year or so. This exceptional retention rate held at about the same level over our initial three years. It was a strong affirmation. I had been in a ton of men's groups for as long as I had been a Christian, and had never seen retention like that.

The second measure was how hard it was to replace members when one left. I didn't want to be constantly in the business of selling new members. Again the results were positive. After about a year, each group solidified and the members began to refer new members for their groups when we had an opening. The existing members became great advocates because they were receiving real value and wanted to share it with friends and others they would nominate to have a seat around the table.

The third metric was the most important. Was there measurable, eternal fruit being produced in the lives of the members and their businesses due to their participation in C12? This was the real home run. Members were seeing the same kinds of fruit in their businesses that we had seen in the Mack Company. People were being saved through business relationships that were a normal part of doing business. Believers were being encouraged to grow in their personal spiritual lives, and countless others were helped by works of love, service, and blessings in the name of Jesus. I was humbly ecstatic. I knew that only God produces eternal fruit, and He was doing it through C12.

After two years I became convinced that the model would be successful in other places. I had designed it to be replicable, and I wanted it to grow. It seemed only logical to me that if C12 was producing transformation and fruitfulness in 36 members across Central Florida, God would want to do the same in Chicago, Atlanta, and Dallas. So I wrote a business plan and began to make overtures to a few contacts in other cities. But my efforts went nowhere. This puzzled me. I was willing to give the idea away or share it for a small fee. I began to pray, asking God why C12 wasn't growing. I didn't get a direct answer that I remember, but I do recall sitting at my desk looking at the business plan when I received an impression. *Lay it down and watch Me grow it.* So I stopped trying to reach out to find associates, and began a wonderful three-year period of personal spiritual training. During that time I learned much about myself, contentment, and grace.

I realized that one of the reasons I wanted C12 to grow was to prove that I had been right, and FCCI was wrong to turn the C12 model down. It was selfish pride, and even though it wasn't the most negative of misguided motivations, it was still ugly and unacceptable to God for a leader of His business. I repented when He revealed my sin, and I actually went to FCCI and asked forgiveness. I also learned that contentment is a choice that we make, based on a real understanding of God's Grace. We truly deserve nothing from God but to die and go to hell. And when we look closely at what we've been given in our salvation with all of His provision and care, we realize that we neither deserve, nor can we demand, any of it. He has given us all we need and so much more. To *not* be thankful and content is to shake our fist in the face of God and, like a spoiled child, shout "I want more!"

When I laid down my hope to grow C12, I began to look honestly at what I had already been given. I'd gained almost 40 members that I really loved to work with and who responded to me as friends. I had an income that was more than adequate to meet my family's needs. All of my contacts were within a 90-mile radius of our home, and the materials and format for the C12 concept were producing exciting, eternal fruit as well as great business results.

When I considered these things, I was humbled and broken. How could I honestly look at all I had been given and tell God it wasn't enough? No, I had more than enough—more than I deserved, and all freely given by God. I chose contentment as the result of the realization of this truth. I can remember saying to God in prayer; "Father, I can never thank You enough for what I have. I don't care if C12 never grows beyond the three groups that You have given me. I love what I do, and I am so very grateful. I don't even deserve this, let alone have the right to ask for more. Thank You."

Grace is defined as unearned favor, and I certainly had experienced that in so many ways. I realized that contentment is a choice we make to trust God and to accept what we have as best for us. He gives to us from His love, in total harmony with His eternal plan for our lives. We will always have all we need to do all He wants. Happiness and joy only exist in the present moment, and our attitude towards our circumstances reveals our hearts towards that truth. Always wanting more is an affront to God's love and equates to telling Him that He doesn't love us enough to give us what we really need. Discontent is the opposite of trust in God.

It seemed that when I reached contentment and stopped trying to grow C12 in my own timing, God released C12 to grow. I know that doesn't make much sense, but that's what happened. When I came to the point where I was content with what God had provided and really didn't want to grow, we began to grow. I soon witnessed His provision in many ways.

First, I had been invited to speak to a ministry group in California, and asked a member to fill in by facilitating one of Florida's groups for me. It was the only time I ever did that. When I returned and we debriefed about his experience in leading the group, he said, "You know, that was fun. I think I would rather do what you do than what I do." That member, Scott Hitchcock, the owner of a successful leadership training franchise in Tampa, was a perfect choice to be the first one to test my theory. We worked out a way for him to transition over the next six months while he sold his business to a successor. That done, he joined C12 as our first Territory Chair in 1997. He's still serving in that role 17 years later. As of this writing, Scott is the longest serving of our 64 C12 Chairs and is the namesake of C12's highest annual Chair award, The Hitchcock Chair of the Year.

Several other leaders followed Scott, including our first female Chair, Diana Furr, who started a group in Washington, DC. Within three years we added several more territories, with C12 Groups launching in Ocala, Virginia Beach, Tampa, Los Angeles, Phoenix, Chicago, Dallas, Washington (DC), and Grant's Pass (Oregon). Of course we had a few stumbles along the way, but it became clear that C12 could grow to be a real business. The Chairs who came forward were all led by God's Spirit. We had not reached out in the prior three years, yet in the course of years two and three, we added *seven* new Chairs and metro areas to serve.

I was thrilled with the progress, but over time I began to resist the idea of further growth. I was happy to write the materials and lead the three groups I had started with, but I felt that more people in C12 leadership could complicate my life and require more of my time to serve them. I realized that I might actually miss the days of small beginnings and the intimate friendships I had with the C12 members I was serving. But Jesus made it quite clear: We were to grow and we were to do it right.

I began discussions with my Board—all founding C12 members—about the vision for C12 to become a real business. Early in 1999, I asked them to do two things to lay the foundation for our future growth. First, I asked them to agree to meet monthly as a group for a season. Second, that we attend "The Vision of a Leader" conference in Atlanta. As I outlined my vision for what I termed "an engaged, collegial Board of Directors," two of them said they couldn't make the commitment and resigned. The remaining five members and I attended the conference in the fall of 1999.

Throughout the conference, we stayed together and prayed together. We did the 16-hour drive together and met often for prayer and discussion during the three days of the event. We asked ourselves, "Is C12 of God?" and, "Is it man's idea, or God's?" As we reviewed how we started and all that God had done to supply, protect, and grow C12 along with the tangible, eternal fruit, it was obvious that only God could have done it. We then asked ourselves, "If C12 is of God, where would He *not* want it to go?" And, "Which Christian business owners would He *not* want to have the opportunity to participate?" It seemed clear that if God birthed C12 and He proved it to be helpful and valuable in a few cities, He would want it made available in all cities, everywhere. We felt that we needed to have a world vision perspective on C12's future.

At that time I was 61 years old, and realized that as stewards we should begin the process of planning for C12's long-term leadership succession. We began a rudimentary search for a younger successor. We also decided to plan for the release of my three initial groups to new leaders so I could focus on building an infrastructure to support the expansion we believed was about to happen. It was truly a seminal time in the history of the The C12 Group, and also in my life.

Returning home, we began to pray for God's timing and provision of the right people to buy my groups, and for my successor as well. I asked my group members to pray along with me, and they kiddingly refused! They didn't want me to leave them. They had become my closest friends and most trusted brothers and sisters. But they saw the Lord's hand clearly leading C12 and agreed to pray. The process of transition had begun!

In 2001, I sold my three groups: one to Scott Hitchcock in Tampa, and the other two—in Sarasota and Bradenton—to Don Light. I had always believed that while the relationship between the C12 Chair and the group was special and important, the real value for the members was the group itself. My theory was about to be tested.

I sold the groups on a time-purchase plan with a three- to four-year payout that would provide income for Bonnie and me. That way, I could focus on building a structure to better train and support our Chairs and strengthen our brand. C12's overall income wasn't sufficient to provide us with a salary at that point. If we were wrong and it didn't grow, we would "eat our seed corn." We had very little savings and no other source of income at the time. And of course, if the groups fell apart under the new leaders, the seed corn wouldn't be there either. But God provided again. None of the groups lost a single member in the first two years after the transfer. Truly, the value of the group *was* the group.

Administration is not my gift. Actually, I detest it. While we did make progress by improving our materials and setting up a website, it was clear that C12 needed someone with different gifts and the passion to take it to the next level. I was blessed to have had a member, John Peter, who owned a graphics design business. He was a great help, giving me excellent advice and service for many years.

I started supplying the new Chairs with monthly materials for a very reasonable flat fee, and supplied them with binders, business cards, and stationery—all at no cost. We started drawing the Chairs together twice each year for fellowship and training. We began holding annual C12 Leadership CEO Conferences in Florida, and were able to offer them at a profit. Our concept was to invite members who did something in their businesses or ministry particularly well, to present at these conferences, to teach and inspire other members, based on their own hard-earned and extremely credible and relevant practices and experiences. It has been a wonderful innovation, and the members have continued to be a great resource for each other. Amazingly, we were able to have nationally known Christian CEOs, who "get" business as a ministry, featured as keynote speakers—men such as Norm Miller of Interstate Batteries and Bill Pollard of Service Master. All in all, the C12 business grew, but it was a labor of duty for me since I knew I was not the man best suited for this role.

Once, when I was writing the original business plan for C12 and analyzing the different talents and abilities that would be needed to fulfill the vision and make C12 a world-class organization, I became a bit overwhelmed. I realized I didn't have a fraction of what would be needed— neither financially, nor in terms of the variety of talents— to grow C12 into a world-class organization able to support those called to honor God. As I reflected over C12's needs and thought about what it might become, I heard God whisper to me: *All you need is in the Body of Christ and I will bring it to you when you need it.* No, I didn't really hear an audible voice. But those of you who know Him know exactly what I mean. Those of you who don't know Christ won't get it, no matter how I try to explain it. But I heard that still, small voice almost 20 years ago, and I have had the honor to see Him do exactly what He said He would do. Today, C12 has grown to over 1,500 members and operates in 30 states. And everything about C12 continues to improve and strengthen each year through God's providence.

Chapter 12

The Value of a Believing Wife

Before I close, I want to give credit to my wife, Bonnie. Without her as my partner throughout this whole life experience, C12 would never have happened. The lack of materialistic desire on Bonnie's part and her patient willingness to always trust God to provide for us were priceless assets to me. Not only has she constantly prayed for me and lifted me and C12 up to God, but there were times when I was down and ready to quit, and she encouraged me. She often said, "No, you can't quit. This is what God has called you to do and He will keep us going. Just keep trusting Him." She always reminded me that there's really no worthy life lived apart from God's will, and no real happiness outside of His order.

When a husband and wife are not in unity, they can't be moving forward together as one, as in "the two shall become one." There will always be tension between them. The foundational priority of marriage has always been fundamental to our overall philosophy in C12. I believe that a successful marriage is more important to God than a successful business, and that in Him the best is not "either/or," but "both/and" for an integrated life lived in His order. As part of this perspective, The C12 Group has a strategic alliance with Family Life Ministries (a like-minded Christian ministry focused on building healthy marriages and families), which enables us to equip our Chairs and key members to conduct "The Art of Marriage" seminars with the purpose of strengthening marriages within C12 and the Body of Christ. Aside from the marriage seminars, many of our monthly teaching segments include instruction and exhortation to live a life of structure and order within a marriage under the Lordship of Christ.

The marriage relationship is among the highest of God's priorities for life and ministry and has practical and powerful outcomes. After all, what is the value of having a successful business if your marriage is a failure, particularly if the failure is linked to an overcommitment of time and focus building the business? God doesn't give us a business to ruin our marriage. A fundamental mistake we often find among Christian CEOs is a leader who takes all the time they think they need for the business, while trying to fit the needs of their spouse and family into what's left over. That doesn't work. The reverse is far more profitable ... but more about that in a moment.

In C12, we find many of our new members have significant tension in their marriages. Some are actually unhealthy and on the verge of breaking up. This should be no surprise when we consider the statistical likelihood of divorce in our culture, even among Christians. Often, through their interaction with the C12 curricula and the other members, they recognize (perhaps for the first time) that a godly marriage is possible. They become aware that they can do better, and through the encouragement of their peers and the accountability that their group provides, they do, and they start towards marriage as God intends. When that happens, wives testify and God smiles.

***

Before I was saved in 1973, I had been married and divorced twice. Apparently, I was an expert in making a marriage fail! Nineteen seventy-three was the same year I met Bonnie and we fell in love ... or what we thought was love. We've learned through the years a much deeper and more meaningful definition. Anyway, in April of 1974 we were married. In 1975 our first daughter, Sarah, was born. Leah joined us in 1977. My daughter, Beth, from my first marriage, fell in love with Jesus in 1975.

Sometime during 1975, I found myself feeling some of the restlessness that had contributed to my previous marriage failures. But things had changed for me since then. I was a Christian now and divorce was not an option. I struggled for a bit, and finally got on my knees and prayed. I asked God, "What's wrong, Father? Why can't I find the happiness and fulfillment in marriage that I hoped for? Why am I unable to make it work?" I heard Him say in my spirit, *The problem is in you, Buck. You are looking to someone else for something you can only find in Me.*

I was startled, to say the least. I had justified both of my failures to be the fault of my former wives. I blamed them for our problems. As I reflected, I realized the truth: God was right. Neither of my previous failed relationships was necessary. Each of my former wives was a fine woman who tried hard to make our marriage work, and the fault was mine alone. It was hard to swallow, but I knew it was true. What to do now?

I went to Bonnie, confessed my revelation, and we prayed together seeking direction. We read the fifth chapter of Ephesians and talked about what living out God's commands to husbands and wives might look like in our relationship. We prayed and told God we wanted to have the marriage that He intended for us; we wanted to become *one* in the fullest sense of what He intended. We each promised we would do whatever it took to get there. This was a key step and the real starting point of our Christ-centered marriage. We had recited the traditional vows on our wedding day, but only now did we begin to deeply understand what they meant and commit to truly honor them.

Of course, our marriage relationship hasn't been perfect. But we have both committed to growing together in the ways of God and His design for us for nearly 40 years. At this point I would like to be able to say that we finished our successful marriage project years ago, and that we're now simply enjoying the fruit of our labor. But that's not true because we're still working on our marriage. Building a successful marriage takes continual intention, attention, repentance, and prayer.

The nurture and love of a believing spouse has been a priceless asset to me and is an absolute essential for the well-being of our businesses, our personal peace and fulfillment, and most of all, our witness for the Kingdom of God. When you think about it, there really is no better alternative, is there?

Throughout our 40 years together, Bonnie and I have grown through falling in love and marrying, birthing babies, parenting teenagers, graduating them from college, marrying them into new families, and now relating to them as friends and counselors. We're also grand-parenting six grandchildren between the ages of five and 24. We have changed and our love has changed as we have passed through the many stages of life to become senior citizens. Our marriage is the best it has ever been, but it still takes focus and intentionality.

The law of entropy seems to be at work in our lives, always pushing back against anything that will lead to obedience or experiencing God's best for us.

It is by God's Grace that we have pressed on and not been willing to settle for "good enough." If we compare our marriage to others, we look pretty good, and by the world's standards we've done well. Still, in a bell curve distribution of all marriages, half will fail. Many stay together for convenience, finances, fear, shame, or for the sake of the children. But the measure for us has not been to be "good enough" or above average, but rather *God's best* marriage as He created it to be. His will is for us to love as He designed, and to express together all we can through all the phases and stages of life, as in "the two shall become one." We aren't there yet, but we press on. We believe it is God's will not only for us, but for every Christian couple.

You know, we change as we mature, and what love might have looked like at 25 or 35 looks very different at 75. But God is the same and His will for us is always for His best. Aging is part of life and we change in many ways as we pass through it. But love—God's love—doesn't change. His way for us is always best in all of our relationships, especially in the unique central relationship of marriage.

Of all our responsibilities as Christian leaders, the imperative to grow in and model a God-honoring marriage is second only to our responsibility to nurture and grow in our intimacy with and knowledge of God and His ways. In fact, we cannot do one without the other. If we are growing closer to God, we will be growing closer to our God-given mates. To build a successful business and at the same time be in a failed marriage is not coherent with God's plan for us.

C12 is committed to doing all we can to be a godly influence that enables success in both business and marriage. Obviously, it takes two parties—actually three—to make marriage work. And, unfortunately, it's possible for any of us to do all we can and still experience marriage failure. But failure will never be God's best. May we commit together that, for us, God's best is, and will forever be, our goal. Not just survival, not to be better than average, but His best. "For me and my house, we will serve the Lord" (Joshua 24:15).

In our current culture, marriage is among the godly practices that the world disdains and attempts to marginalize out of existence. Our nation and the world desperately need to see models of marriages lived out as God created and intended for them to be, as His very best for life as a couple. He really doesn't have a plan B.

May God grant us His strength and Grace to run through the tape together with our spouse, finish strong, and let His Light shine through us as we do.

Chapter 13

C12 Grows as God Supplies

In the fall of 2001, I received a phone call on a Saturday from a man who introduced himself as Don Barefoot. He was from Greensboro, North Carolina, and he told me he had heard about C12 and was interested to learn more about it. He said, "I know that you don't know me, but I think maybe I'm supposed to help C12." He told me how he had very recently learned of C12 through Ralph Miller, our Chair in Virginia Beach. I couldn't help but think, *This could be the man God is calling to replace me, to lead C12 to the next level.* But on reflection, it seemed impossible, since we had no money to even begin to pay an executive with Don's résumé. He had his own general management consulting practice, had been CEO of very large companies, was an elder in a solid evangelical church, and was an MBA graduate of MIT's Sloan School of Management. Don and his wife were visiting relatives in the Tampa Bay area at the time. He said he could visit me anytime during the next week. We agreed to meet at my home on Monday. We hit it off instantly. I told the Board about our conversation and asked them to pray for our meeting. Don visited on Monday and we spent a day together sharing our testimonies and visions, talking about C12, our Board, and how it all worked. We even played a round of golf together. Then I invited Don to visit our Tampa group meeting as a guest. He did, and you know the rest of the story as I related it in the prologue. Don saw how God used the group process in real time. After that meeting, we agreed to talk some more. "Coincidentally," we had a dinner for the C12 Board planned for later in the week, and with the Board's approval I invited Don and his wife, Karen, to join us.

The Board meeting in our home was informal and pleasant, and we all came away with a lot to think about. We had some discussions among the Board members and concluded that the only way we could hope to move forward with Don would be for him to start a C12 Group in Greensboro. This would also demonstrate his commitment to the work and build important first-hand experience with our model. He would also continue to consult with select clients, as he had done in the past. That way he could continue to meet his financial needs, and we would have time to get to know each other better, and pray for God's guidance.

I think we were all amazed when he agreed to start groups in Greensboro and lead them while we worked to flesh out and fund a plan for growth. We had never had a presence in the Carolinas prior to this time. Don began leading his first C12 Group in May 2002, and quickly built to two C12 Groups and a C12 Key Players Group. In the decade since then, C12's Carolina presence has grown to 12 Chairs leading 25 groups, with nearly 300 members today. In the spring of 2003, Don agreed to join C12's Board to allow us to work closely together and further develop our relationship while we worked through C12's long-term strategic issues. Later, we added Dave Dunkel (a long-term member leading a $1+ billion public company) and Mark Cress (Founder and Chairman/CEO of Corporate Chaplains of America) to the Board.

In 2004, the Board asked Don to prepare a strategic plan for the transition of C12 from the "mom and pop" leadership that Bonnie and I had been providing, to a more robust and sustainable structure and business model. The plan included the transfer of the C12 Home Office to Greensboro, under Don's leadership. Don agreed, and at our spring 2004 meeting, the Board adopted his plan, which included raising $260,000 in investment cash to capitalize The C12 Group, LLC, to be able to fund the critical next 18 months.

We initially thought we would need to raise more capital after this formative time period. The Board felt that they should be the first to risk investment in C12, and they each committed to a portion of the $260,000 that God put in their heart and according to their ability. It is now 10 years later, and we have not had to raise another cent. God has supplied all we need to do all He has asked, adding yet another testimony to His sovereign supply.

Part of that original capital was used to begin to pay me a modest salary which, prior to that time, we were unable to do. The business had previously paid Bonnie a very small salary as bookkeeper, and we lived on the proceeds of the sale of my three groups. We had about $40,000 in the bank, which we transferred into the new account. Don and the Board insisted that I be paid a reasonable salary since the business needed to stand on its own as a business, and because I was to continue as CEO for a season and remain active.

I mention all of this—the capitalization, the investors' agreement, etc.—because this was God's way of allowing me to realize a dream that I had for years. After I left the Mack Company and was working as a consultant to my friend's business, I had been challenged to describe an "ideal" Christian company. I had invested a lot of time and prayer in thinking through the ins and outs of the concept, and had actually written a paper that described the fundamentals of a Christian business. It began with a system of shared ownership and authority within the structure of the business. My model was the New Testament church as it is described in the Bible (not necessarily how we see it practiced today). The principle of multiple leaders with co-equal authority—described as "elders," or "overseers"—was the key.

I had seen several ministry businesses start well and then fail because of the indiscretions or bullheaded mistakes of a founder who never released personal control of the organization. In my opinion, that is why the Word always speaks of elders in the plural. I had dreamed of how one person could start a business and then as it grew, distribute ownership to key leaders who would share authority through a process of "selective addition." Since the owner would be naturally very slow to hire a key person with whom he would share his ownership and authority, this would clearly require hearing from God. The world would scoff at the idea, but God's way is not defined by the world's thinking.

As we worked through the original C12 investment structure, I insisted that we adopt a governance model that gave one seat on the Board to each investor, regardless of the percentage of ownership they held. In addition, I urged that we adopt a policy whereby every decision requiring a Board vote must be unanimous. So while I maintained the majority of the stock, I would effectively give my ability to control the business to the Board of Directors operating in prayerful unity. That was a radical idea indeed! In business, who voluntarily gives up control? After much prayer and discussion, we unanimously agreed to adopt corporate bylaws that require Board unity in all Board decisions.

God used me to start C12, but it has always been His. So when the time came to give it up to others and share authority and responsibility with them, it was easy. To date, our operations have never been impeded by our covenant to be in total unity. It may take a bit longer to make some decisions, but I have no doubt that the decisions we've made have been better decisions. That is because in leading C12, there has been a humility and submission to God and to one another that we would have lost in other environments. Our Board is God's gift to me. I could never have imagined that accomplished, God-fearing men like Martin Newby, Darryl Lanker, Mark Dillon, Mark Cress, Dave Dunkel, and Don Barefoot would join in the vision of C12 and commit to seeking God's will for its future with me. I am in awe of each of them and at God's provision in, and through, them. These men initially committed to meet monthly for a season to guide us in the transition stage, and we have settled into a quarterly Board meeting schedule in the years since then.

We moved the office from our home to a new location in Greensboro, North Carolina, and Don joined officially as President and COO in January of 2005. He then became CEO in July of 2006. Under his wise leadership, we have grown steadily. We now have 65 Chairs and 1,500 total members. Amazingly, we estimate that these members routinely interact with more than 2½% of the U.S. adult population who are "stakeholders" of these companies in various forms (employees, customers, suppliers, trade associates, etc.) … quite a substantial mission field! Billings through the Chairs are now approximately $12,000,000 annually.

We have chosen to stay focused on North America until we're sure that we have identified God's chosen partners in other countries—leaders who we are able to unite within the Spirit as well as the work.

One critical component of C12 that means so much to me, and which confirms God's guiding and providential hand in C12, is our amazing group of Chairs. That goes for our equally amazing Home Office staff as well. I have been through organizational development in several settings in the past, and have been blessed by relationships with some great people.

But I have never seen anything like the group that our Lord has brought together in C12. There is a spirit of harmony, commitment, and love that cannot be forced or mandated. It is God's gift.

Since organizations don't have souls, they cannot be saved. But I do believe there is a personality or spirit—an aroma about them—that is felt more than described. People react to it, sense it, *feel* it. When that personality reflects the love of God in Christ, lacks selfish ambition, and is subservient to the good of the Kingdom, it is palpable and unmistakable. And when you add the active spirit of the C12 members that I've had the privilege to know from all across our country, I am absolutely overwhelmed. I know I have had little to do with it. Yes, God used me to start C12, but I had no idea it would become what it has. Back in 1992 I never knew it was possible at all, let alone what I now sense that C12 could eventually become. People truly are the key to the success of any organization, and God has joined the finest I have ever known to do His work in C12.

Another amazing thing to me is the consistent quality, commitment to Jesus, and fruitfulness of the members of every C12 Group I have visited. One of the basic concerns in the early years was the scalability of the concept. More specifically, could the results that I had seen in the groups I led, be repeated through others who possessed differing gifts, skills, personality types, and so on? The evidence says yes. Through the application of a consistent format, unique materials integrating a biblical worldview and relevant business best practices, and dedicated Chairs, there is quantifiable and consistent fruit beyond my wildest dreams. In 2013 we saw 4,000+ come to salvation through business relationships with C12 member companies, and $150 million given to the cause of Christ. I know that what we have is no accident, but just further proof of God's sovereign provision and that His ways work best. It doesn't matter where in the country I visit or what group, the members are cut from one cloth … the very best of the best. I am awed at what I have experienced and witnessed in them.

C12 is the culmination of my life's work and exceeds my highest hopes and most fervent dreams. I am broken before a God who would choose to use a man like me to do such meaningful work. It is proof of the reality of a loving, redeeming Father who creates and calls the most unlikely of the world to show His Grace and power.

So there you have it—the answer to why I am a radical. Radically saved by a radical God whose radical love sent His Son to a tree to die in my place and give me a new life, a new start. Early on, I heard it said that "The world has yet to see what God can do through one man whose heart is fully surrendered to Him." I am not that man, but I have wanted to be.

Nothing in this world can compare with walking with Jesus. I have tried it all and can't compare. How about you? Anyone can be a radical. All it takes is one prayer: "Jesus, I'm all in!"

Chapter 14

What's Next? – A Message from Don Barefoot, C12's President and CEO

As Buck recounted earlier, my introduction to The C12 Group came in a totally unexpected and unplanned way that instantly stirred something deep inside me. I've since come to understand my reaction to discovering that an organization like C12 even existed, as Christ within me resonated like a tuning fork to something of His own design. At the time, though, in late 2001, I was excited but cautious … concerned I might be disappointed that C12 wasn't of sufficient quality, intensity, or impact.

Less than two years before this time, at the age of 46, I had left a 20-year career as CEO or COO of a series of five increasingly larger global leadership companies to have more freedom to serve Christ as an elder in my local Bible-centered church, while advising other CEOs in my sweet spot (large manufacturing and marketing companies) to lead more effectively. From when I was very young, the Lord had given me exceptional opportunities to learn and gain leadership experience. I had managed people in a corporate setting from the age of 19 onward, and had been given a topflight business education and an early opportunity to see and reject complacent, politically correct corporate leadership (General Motors). I then took the plunge, as a very young executive, in a Fortune 100 company known as an ideal training ground for future CEOs (Emerson Electric). For His own sovereign reasons, the Lord provided me with these experiences and capabilities at an early age, before later giving me a vibrant, all in, Christ-centered faith.

Although I had thought of myself as a Christian from my youth—due to being churched in a mainline denomination—I came to a saving faith in Christ at the age of 40. Sure, I had previously been baptized, confirmed, involved in Sunday school and youth retreats, served the least among us, taught Sunday school, and served as an altar boy. But sadly, I had never heard the real Gospel of Christ. I didn't truly know God's Word or understand it to be totally inerrant and inspired. I also hadn't seen myself as a fallen sinner incapable of restoration with our Holy God outside of the perfect life, sacrifice, and resurrection of Jesus on my behalf. In short, like many American "Christians," I had never sat under true biblical teaching and didn't know Christ as Savior and Lord. I had embraced "Jesus plus ..." thinking. Unfortunately, this is so typical in America, where only 30% of adults are regular churchgoers and just half of them attend true biblical churches that teach salvation by faith in Christ alone.

Joining my first Bible-centered church changed everything. Challenged by God's Word, I came to the end of myself once the Lord patiently allowed me to wrestle with the historicity of the Genesis account. While studying history, archaeology, astrophysics, and microbiology to prove the biblical account to myself, my God-wired propensity to see truth through statistical confirmation kicked in. After several weeks of wrestling with God and gathering relevant data, the score was God's Word, 200, and secular worldview, zero! Finally, I was able to get on my knees and confess what I now knew to be true. Little did I realize the wild ride onto which I was about to embark, given this total recalibration of what it meant to abide in Christ with eternity in mind. My prior notions of "servant leadership"—rooted in situational ethics and man-centered philanthropy—were replaced by a new accountability and hope rooted in God's Grace and the pursuit of His truth and eternal purpose. My new mission was to become a trustworthy steward and ambassador for Christ, speaking the truth in love while pursuing God's highest in light of a biblical worldview.

Like so many C12 members, I was an adult convert who could now better distinguish between living and leading with integrity under a moralistic, man-centered notion of Christian ethics (i.e., comparative righteousness), and actually living as a 24/7 follower of Christ under submission to God's living and inspired Word. This vital difference is what fuels Christ-centered ministry. It is the very reason C12 exists to equip Christian CEOs, and it literally separates darkness and death from light and eternal life.

The "old" Don toiled for money under the world's constantly changing laws and ethics, while attempting to be the sovereign provider (a living insurance policy) for his family and future family generations. The "new" Don worked with excellence as unto the Lord under the higher, timeless standards of our unchanging, sovereign, and trustworthy God, who—as Creator and Provider—is more than able to sustain His children. He gave us His Word so that (1) we would know enough about Him, His purpose and plan, to realize our need for a redeemer, and (2) that His plan includes us (Ephesians 2:10) and the resources and opportunities He entrusts to us (e.g., Psalms 24:1, Matthew 25:14–30, Luke 19:11–27, 1 Corinthians 15:58, Colossians 3:23, Philippians 4:19). I now know we trust and abide in Christ as we strive to live based on God's eternal perspective, recognizing that our heavenly future is impacted by what we do while "in the body" (2 Corinthians 5:10).

By my mid-forties, I was growing like a weed in my new biblical Christian faith, and found myself more stretched and challenged in my role as church elder than I was as a "turn-around" chief executive of yet one more company. Solid biblical discipling at our church, combined with completing Bible Study Fellowship's seven-year curriculum, had opened my eyes to the possibilities of living larger for the cause of Christ. So I left the helm of a multibillion-dollar company with 30,000 employees, and began a general management consulting practice to selectively work with a handful of major clients at a time. This was the first time I had operated independent of a large corporation and it truly was my first experience in leading a small business.

My wife was relatively comfortable as a CEO's wife and was sure that I'd soon be swept off my feet by the next billion-dollar enterprise in need of a turn-around CEO. She watched and waited as I passed on several such opportunities, and then saw the Lord slam the door shut on the one large public company needing a turnaround that I would actually consider. A larger public firm had acquired it in a hostile takeover. Actually, this was a relief. Even though I would have approached the job as an openly evangelical

Christian CEO, I truly believed the Lord had something else for me in this next season that would stretch me and multiply my efforts as His disciple.

I found myself enjoying the role of advisor to CEOs and soon realized that each of my public company CEO clients were Christians. I also learned that I was just as focused on encouraging them and holding them accountable to be godly servant leaders as I was on advising them on ways to sharpen their business model and performance.

Later, while in Virginia Beach to consider the possibility of doing doctoral work to sharpen my consulting craft, I was confronted by the Entrepreneur-in-Residence on the staff of Regent University's Christian graduate business school. He looked me square in the eye and told me that investing a couple years pursuing higher education would be a waste of time, given my background and future focus. He said, "You should check this out," and put his C12 Chair's notebook in front of me. It turns out that Professor Ralph Miller had previously built and sold two companies and was now lecturing MBA students while also leading a C12 practice in the Tidewater area of Virginia (this was a few years prior to C12's full-time requirement for incoming Chairs). After flipping through Ralph's C12 notebook for a few moments, I began to get excited. I made a mental note to look up Buck Jacobs the next time we visited our extended family in the Tampa Bay area.

Meanwhile, as I wondered how to best serve Christ, given my business leadership background, Buck and his C12 Board had been earnestly praying for several months that the Lord would bring them a successor to follow Buck in leading and building The C12 Group into the next decade. Buck was in his early sixties at the time. Now, 13 years later, having served as the first C12 Chair in the Carolinas and 10 years as President of C12, I'm 60 and again beginning to openly discuss developing C12's next-generation leadership with our Board while Buck continues to serve well in the role of Board Chairman.

We are blessed in that the Lord has drawn together a Board in which, at 13 years, I have the least C12 tenure. Every Director is devoted to seeing our Lord honored and our clients served well for His glory. The selfless, Christ-centered unity of this group—the only C12 equity holders—is our strongest asset as we look to the future. Although we're structured as an LLC, each

Board Director is serving without any personal agenda or financial urgency regarding their own financial return. Their sole concern is that C12 succeeds in its mission to "change the world by bringing forth the Kingdom of God in the marketplace through the companies and lives of those He calls to run businesses for Him." To address the concerns I stated at the start of this chapter, I saw these qualities in Buck and his Board when we first met, and it was confirmed when I observed my first C12 Group meeting in Tampa in the fall of 2001.

A key driver of C12's effectiveness through the lives and businesses of our members is our uncommon focus: simply serving Christian CEOs and helping them (and those under their care) live fruitful lives from the eternal perspective. It's easy to maintain high standards, coupled with a grace-based, biblical, yet non-prescriptive environment for our members, when this is our only purpose! As we like to say, we're all in and dedicated full-time to our God-given calling as long as He gives us the strength. We're not pursuing the "American dream" of accumulating sufficient material wealth to retire early. We're "sticking to our knitting," and have an intergenerational sense of stewardship through business. In this way, C12 stands in contrast with other organizations that seek to serve Christian CEOs but fail to sustain the necessary focus, excellence, and expectation of what's possible with eternity in mind, which is so necessary to truly serve and encourage these clients towards God's best and highest.

C12's culture is unique. We're all about business, life balance, and God-honoring priorities and purpose. We're biblical, yet focused on applying the essentials of the faith around which Christians can unite, and carefully avoid chasing the many doctrinal "rabbits" that could distract our practical focus. We combine the expectation that leading a company God's way will also tend to produce superior business results—something proven through more than 4,000 C12 members over the past two decades, during both strong and weak economic climates. Our member companies, on whole, vastly outperform their market peers. They're also more resilient during tough times and more likely to avoid complacency or major strategic blunders during good times. At the same time, they learn from each other how to be better ambassadors for Christ and actively minister to company stakeholders through their business processes and like-minded staff. Overall, this results in substantial eternal fruit as we annually see an average of more than four salvations per C12 member company, and many millions of dollars given to support vibrant ministry flowing through the marketplace where the unchurched are much more likely to be reached. The beneficial business and ministry impact of C12 membership—something we call The C12 Difference—is available to any CEO willing to engage in lifelong learning, objective peer input, and healthy accountability.

Contrary to popular opinion, it's still quite legal to cast a godly vision for business and to operate according to biblical core principles in today's marketplace! The legal requirement that all U.S. businesses have, not to be discriminatory in hiring, compensating, and promoting employees (i.e., Title VII of the Civil Rights Act of 1964), is relatively straightforward to comply with.

Given that God is directing C12 and its Board, and that we all view ourselves as stewards (not owners) and "clay in the Potter's hand," I'm quite confident that C12's next 22 years will be just as exciting and fruitful as the last. The Lord clearly fit two unlikely pieces together when he put Buck and me into a close, long-term working relationship. Buck's executive career involved a family business, a series of sales-oriented senior leadership positions in smaller firms, and a variety of experiences in smaller independent churches. My background was almost the opposite: large companies, operations and engineering oriented, and being discipled in denominationally networked churches. But God knew! Our complementary backgrounds add to the breadth and depth of C12 and our ability to better serve the broad variety of business types and Christians that come together under the expansive C12 tent. God wired both of us as "high D" leaders with a tremendous regard for the inerrancy of the Bible and high expectations as to what focused and equipped servant leaders can bring to any organization. The Lord brought us each to saving faith as adults, with clear memories of lessons learned in life and leadership from our former unsaved days. He also wired both of us to be fearless, unflinching exhorters, able to speak the truth in love in encouraging fellow leaders for His eternal purposes. While our "iron sharpening iron" occasionally creates a few sparks, we're absolutely unified on our mutual purpose and focus through C12. God simply birthed us 17 years apart, to work side by side for such a time as this.

Looking forward, it's easy to be excited about what the Lord may do through continuing to grow C12 and its impact. Although our current reach is substantial—2.5% of American adults as stakeholders of C12 member companies—we fully expect to more than double this reach over the next five years, before ultimately getting to a long-term level of 10% of the U.S. population. What an opportunity to see transformation, revival, and healthier, God-honoring businesses and communities across this land!

We've been growing at 20+% annually for many years and are still just scratching the surface of our potential in serving Christian CEOs and communities through our uniquely focused offering. As of this writing, we serve 1,500 members across 33 states through the CEO roundtable industry's finest and most dedicated Chair corps, numbering 65. This represents just 1% of the roughly 150,000 biblical worldview Christian CEOs and owners of established U.S. businesses with sufficient staff to delegate and get away for a day each month to strategically focus on their business. As we survey the landscape, we're currently in just half of the metro areas across North America that could support one or more full-time C12 Chairs in this professional, fee-for-service practice. By 2019, we hope to have more than 140 Chairs serving more than 3,000 members, while routinely reaching more than 5% of the U.S. adult population through the marketplace.

C12's vision is "To see an active global Christian business network of CEOs/Owners, with C12 Groups operating in every metro area." Further, we've shown in several U.S. markets that a full C12 Peer Advisory Board can be formed in towns as small as 25,000 people. Generally, however, we like to see a population of one million or more within a 60-mile radius of each C12 Chair, to enable them to build a robust, three-group practice in a reasonable amount of time.

During recent months, we've been busy building our organization, platform, and toolkit, to facilitate this expansion of scope, with the recognition that this scalable near-term vision still falls far short of what is possible over the longer term. North America is just 5% of the world's population, and we estimate that we can reach half of the world's major metro areas using materials translated into three widely spoken languages: English, Mandarin, and Spanish. Amazingly, there are 50 global metro areas of four million or more people—outside of deeply Marxist or Islamist cultures—that can be served in this way. Over time, our expansion will lead us to a structure that includes regional operating executives to ensure that C12's offerings and services sustain the high level of quality, impact, and long-term client loyalty that we're known for.

Perhaps the most satisfying statistic confirming the impact we're having (besides the obvious business and ministry fruit) is the high level of member satisfaction that surfaces when we survey our members. Overall, our 2013 national member survey rated the C12 experience 9.3 on a 10-point scale, and members overwhelmingly indicated that C12 represented both the highest impact and best value among the wide array of CEO roundtable offerings and strategic coaching services they had previously experienced. C12's Net Promoter Score (NPS, a net measure of customer satisfaction that deducts negative responses from highly positive ones) has been an exceptional 80+ across the multiple times that we have surveyed our members. In contrast, the NPS leader in most market sectors is generally between 50 and 75. We attribute this positive response to our Chair corps, Home Office staff, and Board seeing their C12 work as a way to truly bless those that they're serving—not just as a way to make a living. For this, I'm forever thankful to the Holy Spirit's continuing work in the lives of this group of 80 (and growing) dedicated professionals whom I'm blessed to serve. I'm also excited by the extraordinary quality of many of our younger Chairs and staff members as we look towards the future.

We've found that many long-term C12 members desire to become C12 Chairs once they sell or successfully transfer the leadership of their business to the next generation. This process has occurred multiple times across C12 and will be an important part of transitioning into the future for some of our older, baby boomer Chairs. We also regularly meet ex-CEOs and owners who are looking for ways to serve the Lord and finish strong in this life, those who have no prior knowledge of C12 but appreciate the wisdom and high-value focus of our work. We welcome their inquiries and regularly provide orientations to such candidates.

The process of identifying future C12 Chairs, however, is the subject of much prayer and careful assessment, as they must possess a keen sense of God's calling to this role, in addition to a mature biblical Christian faith and solid general management background. Our Chairs must be peers with our members, and must also participate in our regular Chair training events. This develops the skills necessary to effectively facilitate the peer advisory group one-on-one, and workshop processes that are integral to serving our members. Overall, our high standards and expectation for the role of a C12 Chair as a full-time vocation with a business as ministry focus, leads us to talk with roughly 70 candidates for every one that ultimately trains to become part of C12's "Cadre of the Called." In God's economy, we can't settle for less. Best of all, we know that He will provide everything we need to accomplish everything He asks of us.

I'd like to wrap up this brief look at the future of C12 by expressing thankfulness and joy for what we see our Lord doing through so many whom we have the privilege of meeting and serving through business. It's a delight nearly comparable to that of witnessing others receive Christ as Lord and Savior, when the light bulb goes on and Christian CEOs begin to see that their business is their primary God-given ministry. Soon, they begin, in tangible ways, to realize that they have many ongoing opportunities to model a life of faith and share "the life that is truly life" (1 Timothy 6:19) with those they serve. We agree with Billy Graham's assessment that "one of the next great moves of God is going to be through believers in the workplace." Amen, and Godspeed!

Other Books by Buck Jacobs

A Light Shines Bright in Babylon, 2012

Roadmap to Success (Chapter contributions by Buck Jacobs), 2010

A Strategic Plan for Ministry, 2007